Cops Don't Cry:

A book of help and hope for police families

Vali Stone

Resources for Personal Growth & Enhanced Performance

Published by Creative Bound Inc.
Box 424, Carp, Ontario
Canada K0A 1L0
(613) 831-3641

ISBN 0-921165-62-5
Printed and bound in Canada
© 1999 Vali Stone, reprint 2001,2002

Book design by Wendelina O'Keefe
Cover image © PhotoDisc

Canadian Cataloguing in Publication Data

Stone, Vali
        Cops don't cry : a book of help & hope for police families

ISBN 0-921165-62-5

        1. Police—Family relationships.   2. Police—Job stress.
3. Police psychology. I. Title.

HV7921.S76 1999   363.2'01'9   C99-900388-7

Dedication

With love to Paul, my greatest friend, without whose
loyal dedication to his family and work, and his great
sense of humor, this book could not have been written.

To Trevor, who offers us the sun each evening,
filling us with joy and promise.

To Michelle who offers us the moon each morning,
filling us with serenity and hope.

Acknowledgments

The author wishes to acknowledge the support and encouragement received from the many enthusiastic people who believed in this project and helped to see it through.

This book is especially written for all police spouses around the world, who truly deserve the recognition for being the strength and backbone of a very special family unit.

For all police officers, who are our friends, neighbors, lovers, partners, sons and daughters, and especially our heroes, for they are the ones who dedicate and risk their lives daily. May God always protect them.

A special thank you to my parents, Renato and Delia Pivato, who always saw the best in us and taught us by their loving example that anything is possible if you really try.

To my brothers Paul and Eugene, for their passionate faith in me and in all human nature.

To Doug and Pat Stone, Paulanne, Joshua, Rachel, Michele, Derek, Diane, Alana, Kevin, Tracey, Peter, Scott, Mathew, David, Michael, Peter and Geoff for their commitment and devotion.

To my sister, Dolores Greco, who walks hand in hand with me for all eternity.

To my dear friends, Alice, Donna, Debbie and Wendy, who have shared and given their everything over the years, accepting my quirks with love and humor.

To all the officers of the Toronto Police Service, who willingly opened their doors to reveal the fascinating world in which they work, and especially to Chief Dave Boothby and his wife Gloria for their encouragement and support.

To Gail Baird, Barb Clarke and Wendy Bennitz at Creative Bound, along with editor Janet Shorten and designer Wendy O'Keefe, who offered a great amount of energy and direction. And a special thanks to author and friend Dianne Collier, who once said that I should follow my dream.

Contents

Introduction

Policing is a consuming profession with incredibly high elements of stress. Research suggests that police divorce rates are more than double the national average of ordinary marriages. The spouse's fear of physical danger, adjusting to shift work, transfers, and changes in the officer's personality are only a few of the contributing factors, but the most crucial problem is the breakdown of communication within the relationship.

From the beginning of the officers' careers they are trained to control their emotions, and thus are accused of being cold-hearted. Spouses agree that law enforcement officers grapple with the real-life horrors on the job and that the bitter belief that 'cops don't cry' is sadly untrue.

The problems that face law enforcement couples are numerous. Some are lucky enough to have encountered only a few of the obstacles discussed in this book, others are just beginning to notice changes in their relationship, and many are desperately struggling to piece together the puzzle of this distinctive lifestyle.

My research began a few years ago, after what started out as a regular get-together at a friend's home. I overheard a conversation between a police officer and another guest. The guest was complaining about the time it took an officer to arrive at the scene of an accident he'd been involved in. His agitation increased as he spilled forth every negative police-related issue he could think of.

The officer continued to smile and politely nod his head in understanding. That's when I noticed a woman push past the officer and stand face to face with the guest. "They do the best they can!" she shouted fiercely, her face crimson and her shoulders bunched forward like tight fists. "I'd like to see you try it for one day! Just one day!" Her husband touched her shoulder and she reluctantly drew back, obviously shaken. "I can't take this any more," she whispered to both men and walked away.

I knew exactly what she was feeling. The two of us discussed our fears and disappointments that evening, but it was her parting comment that sparked the beginning of this book: "I wish I had known what I was getting into before I married him."

"This profession has greatly affected my life and the life of my family" is a statement that is reiterated by many police spouses. By means of interviews, surveys and 20 years of personal experience, it became obvious to me that many of the same problems are evident in all police families and that we have many experiences in common. Spouses and officers of all levels from across Canada and the United States have eagerly offered their heartfelt experiences and knowledge in a genuine desire to assist other police families.

There is an urgent need to educate officers and their families about the joys and pitfalls of this kind of relationship. Police departments are beginning to understand that positive family reinforcement is the key to a happy, healthy and productive police officer.

Mrs. Gloria Boothby, wife of Chief Dave Boothby of the Toronto Police Service, strongly recommends mandatory spousal programs and urges spouses to make an effort to attend. "It will give them a better understanding of what's involved and how to value the relationship and the positive aspects of the job."

As in any relationship, the parties must work hard to maintain a sense of balance, but in a police relationship where there are added stresses, there must be very much a 'team' effort. Through trust, understanding, determination and love, the entire family will reap the rewards of a very challenging and exciting lifestyle.

Throughout the book, I have used "he" when referring to a police officer. But there are many women police officers, as will become clear from the quotations. I do not use the masculine pronoun to exclude women, but for convenience.

Quotations in italics are from the survey I conducted or from interviews with police officers and their spouses.

Cops and Robbers

What could have been a more blissful marriage than an office assistant marrying her boss? The nine-to-five insurance company offered us promises of advancement and stability, and we gradually became comfortable with our duties and the firm's technical jargon. Our first year was rapturous, driving to and from work together and enjoying our meager chicken loaf sandwiches between suppressed giggles and under-the-table tootsies in the cafeteria. We were ecstatically happy, or *so I thought*.

At the beginning of our second year of marriage, discontentment crept up on Paul. At first it was his impatience toward what he considered incompetent co-workers and poor management, but then he became increasingly less tolerant of incidents at work that he once would have simply shrugged off. At home he sat in front of the television, listless and tired. His frustration with work was causing a problem in our relationship. He expressed his need for change, stating his desire for something "more adventurous." He quit work and tried his hand at everything from truck driving to landscaping, self-employment to sales; in fact, he changed jobs 12 times that year. He was so restless and miserable that I began wondering who this man that I had married really was. I looked for other projects to keep me occupied so I wasn't in his way.

We both remember the day that Paul finally recognized his lifelong ambition. He was between jobs when he observed our new neighbor leaving for work, handsomely bedecked in his Toronto Police uniform and bidding his family goodbye. We watched from behind the curtains as he removed his night stick from his belt and his police hat and placed them on the seat of the car. It was just a small, routine act, but it rocked Paul like an earthquake.

"That's when I finally woke up," recalled Paul. "I thought about my childhood, growing up in the small town of Huntsville, where even at the brilliant age of nine I knew what I really wanted to be when I grew up. I ardently revealed to each friend and neighbor that I was going to be a cop and that one day I'd be back to clean up the town. I'm sure they banished any thoughts of that as they watched me struggle through my teenage years, but to everyone's astonishment I continued on to college in the law enforcement field. Upon completion, I was offered a position with the Ontario Provincial Police, which I promptly rejected. It is my greatest regret. I just wasn't prepared to shear my long strands of ginger hair to look like a geek. It wasn't cool in the '70s. But watching that policeman from behind the curtains so many years later, I guess I finally grew up."

Paul's story is not an uncommon one. The spouses who begin their marriage with a partner who has been in the department for a while may already have had a scanty glimpse of what lies ahead. But those who married a nine-to-five man who decides later in the marriage that the police department is for him, look out—life is about to become a fierce tornado! But hang in there. Even though you think your lives will never, ever again seem 'normal', gradually you will begin to develop some unique traits. You will become a master at juggling the calendar, making decisions, acting as sole parent and disciplinarian for long stretches of time, and grandly enforcing all morals and values. You become head nurse, doctor, psychiatrist, maid, plumber, painter, gardener, handyman, cook and, for those who work, you will also be an employee. You will on occasion feel hard done by, frustrated, lonely, alienated and weighed down with all the responsibility on your shoulders.

I started to cry when he told me he was applying to the police department. My dad, my brother and my sister-in-law were all cops. I grew up with the late night phone calls, the shhhh's because Dad was sleeping, the birthday disappointments, and I just didn't want that same lifestyle. I wanted a routine job where I could count on him being home in the evenings and on week-ends like everyone else. I didn't want to sit around all night worrying about him either.

Most of us can't understand why anyone in their right mind would choose police work.

Constables are underpaid, overworked, stressed to the limit, known for high divorce rates and high mortality rates, and they continue to risk their lives daily for people they don't even know. Known as the 'cop's other half', we can't believe that the same gentle giant we married has become this independent, self-respecting, dynamic, tough and keen-for-action machine who deals daily with situations we might only see in our nightmares. In the meantime we are beginning to feel that we can't cope with all of these new changes happening around us and we ask ourselves, "Why, oh, why did I marry a cop?" One thing is for certain, spouses I have spoken with who have been married to a police officer for over 20 years all agree that even though it's a crazy yo-yo bungee-jumping existence, it's never once been *boring*!

So, You've Married a Cop!

As a police spouse, you are embarking on a strange new experience. If you look at it as a challenge rather than a chore and strive to see the positive aspects, you will become an astonishingly flexible, unselfish, humorous, sensitive, exceptionally loving and special person. In fact, many veteran spouses also agree that once you become accustomed to this crazy, zany way of life, you wouldn't change places with anyone in the world (well, maybe sometimes, when he's on midnights, the kids have the flu, you're going into your second migraine and you hear some pretty curious noises coming from the dark innards of your unfinished basement).

This book will allow you to discover that we, as members of police families, share common experiences. Many of us have coped with the same stresses and heartaches, worries and fears, and have still managed to earn the wonderful qualities of perseverance and patience, while maintaining our sanity. We have the wonderful ability to cherish life as it should be cherished, one day at a time.

The survey that I distributed to police spouses asked them numerous questions about their lifestyle. The response was overwhelming and the answers to seven pages of questions had me alternately laughing and crying. They are a true indication of the life we lead. I will refer to the survey and quote responses to questions and excerpts from personal interviews throughout the book. Below is a question that brought numerous positive responses:

What are the advantages of being married to a police officer?

Here's what they said:
- Security
- Forces you to grow up and become an independent individual with strong self-esteem
- Exciting life, never a dull moment
- Enjoy outings together mid-week
- Being with a strong mate who can think on his feet
- Married to someone who is honest and hard-working, whom you can respect and be proud of
- Good benefits and salary

- You learn more about the legal system as it relates to the daily news and the public
- You see life from a different point of view and become more tolerant
- Married to someone who can handle any crisis

Why a Cop?

Many citizens have thoughts of becoming a police officer but are immediately turned off by the shift work, the long hours of court time and overtime, and the idea of being set up as a target by criminals, the public and the media. For others, the idea of becoming a police officer has been hovering dangerously in their subconscious for an interminable amount of time, causing them to feel exasperated and unfulfilled. They continue their present wearisome jobs daydreaming of racing through busy city streets like burning rockets, drawing their guns like Dirty Harry and rescuing the weak and unprotected. For some, the need to apply is more subtle, sailing in during a Sunday roast beef dinner or some other family event.

It happened to my husband at the most unexpected time. We were in the delivery room during the birth of our first child. Brian held new baby Sarah in his arms and told her how much he loved her already and how he would always be there to protect her. He looked over at me and mumbled something about changing jobs for a more secure future, like the police department. In my celestial state I smiled at him, which he took as positive reinforcement. Within a month he received his first letter of acknowledgment along with an interview date. What a shock that was.

When that crackpot idea from this madman you've married is finally announced, you may develop a genuine concern that feels like someone hammering a large nail into the pit of your stomach. That feeling may be due to some negative recollections you've managed to suppress over the years. Let's face it, no matter who you are, you become somewhat unnerved when you hear the sound of those sirens screaming up behind you on the highway. You desperately struggle for some intelligent and imaginative excuse in preparation for the impending ticket, only to realize that the cops are chasing the guy one lane over and two cars up. With a sigh of relief you say to yourself, maybe even with a devious laugh, "Whew! Got away again."

Some of us, having been through the rebellious teenage years where we insolently felt the need to fight for our independence and our individual rights, have probably come into contact with the law on a few occasions and that memory has caused a prickly fear in our subconscious. Others may remember the terrorizing screams of friends shrieking, "SPLIT, THE COPS!!" and hundreds of teenage arms and legs cramming their way through a single doorway. We all know of someone who has had a 'bad' experience with police and may even know of someone who has been jailed.

So you ask him, "Why honey, why a cop?" Somehow you manage a feeble smile because you know it's important to him that you understand his dream. And he responds simply, "I've wanted to be a cop since I was a kid." So you convince yourself that you have secretly always wanted to know a cop and now you will get the chance to have one of your own.

The mother of a police officer asked me, "Do you think people are born with the qualities it takes to be a cop or do they just get that way after they've been on the job a while?" Some experts feel that certain personality types are particularly attracted to police work. The many police spouses I spoke to agreed that their partners *craved* a job that was exciting and physically and mentally challenging, away from the nine-to-five claustrophobic, softly carpeted, quiet office atmosphere.

Despite the officers' regular griping about inside departmental politics and the daily media and public lashing, they really enjoy contending with the never-ending calls of domestic disputes, drug busts, auto accidents, alarms, suicides, violations, beatings and stabbings. In their hunger for action they subconsciously learn tolerance and discipline.

Kevin used to listen to a friend of ours tell some pretty gruesome stories while he worked for the New York Police Department. He was so riveted to the conversation that I had difficulty distracting him and at the flirty age of 21, that was scary. He decided he wanted to leave his mundane job in carpet and flooring sales for one where there was action. I went into panic mode. I tried convincing him that the stories he'd been hearing were exaggerated and the job was too dangerous. I threatened to give back his engagement ring. I did not want to get into that kind of marriage. It took a while before I felt comfortable with his decision but I knew if I didn't support him it would cause some serious problems in our relationship.

Routine—What's That?

Many of us lead a pretty routine-oriented life, beginning our day at our place of work with the usual cup of coffee, greeting our co-workers and sharing a few morsels of gossip before attending to the endless piles of paperwork and telephone calls. We take our breaks and lunches at approximately the same time each day. Then we go home to begin our evening routine.

A patrol officer starts his shift never knowing what it will bring. His only regular routine consists of dressing in uniform, collecting the tools of his trade—gun, handcuffs, night stick and so on—and then attending parade where he is inspected and his equipment is checked before his shift begins. He claims the keys for the police vehicle where, once inside, he powers up the police radio, computer terminal, siren and public announcement system and tests the emergency lights. He wheels out onto the street—and that's where his routine ends. He must now psychologically gear himself up for the unknown. There is no warning for what lies ahead and only his previous instruction and experience will help prepare him. This is the beginning of the development of his sixth sense.

Paul describes police work as being like a childhood 'hide and seek' game. You never know who or what is around the next corner and it is the unknown that's so electrifying. He was one of those kids that performed a great many death-defying acts and dares for the sheer pleasure of the adrenaline rush. A good rugged game of cowboys and Indians or cops and robbers was exhilarating. He jumped 50 feet from a bridge into ice-cold water, sat in the gridwork of a train trestle 75 feet over a river and six inches beneath the rails of a passing train just to get a rush. He admits that he was always a spontaneous thrill-seeker. When he recognized his desire to enter police work early in our marriage, I instinctively knew he had finally chosen a job that was right for him.

The majority of the officers' duties are in fact "social service." Other experts feel that police officers develop certain police traits once they're on the job and it's the variety of duties that mold the officer. Their initial draw to the job is an irrefutable need to help people, to perform a great service to their community. They have an acute sensitivity to protect and give assistance to the public, at the same time maintaining their personal strength and authority in a respectable line of work.

Officers consider their work to be as valuable as that of a doctor or nurse, with the added benefit of outdoor freedom. They can act as a psychiatrist or a physician, a phone directory or a city map, a tour guide or a cab driver. A patrol officer will spend the majority of his working hours on the street and the rest in the office and in court.

People will cry to him, spit on him, shoot at him, punch and slap him and lie to him, yet he continues to value the lives of the public above his own. As civilians, we lead our quiet existence and any emergency situation can throw us into despair or panic. A police officer learns to deal with those kinds of situations calmly and reasonably so that we can be put at ease. Thanks to his uniformed presence, his professional, reassuring manner and his authoritive monotone voice, we become less anxious and more confident that we are in capable hands. Those are pretty big shoulders that we are welcomed to lean on. Police officers take their job to protect the public as seriously as protecting their own family.

Interested applicants may choose police work for the job security and the financial benefits that it provides. When a young couple commence their first steps toward a new future together, an officer's starting salary looks remarkably inviting. But make no mistake, he earns every penny of it. The reality of police work is recognized in a very short time. The officer soon learns that he is always on public display and continually up for criticism. This is a raw realization to both the officer and his family. Suddenly, they are a model for society.

I always felt that because Kevin was a cop I had to be more conscientious. I felt guilty if I left the car parked on the street or the kid's tricycles on the sidewalk. I tried to remember to bind my newspapers so that they didn't blow around and was careful not to get into any police-related discussions with friends or neighbors. I was afraid they'd be quick to point a finger at us. I remember a complaint by one neighbor that our basketball net, which was erected on our property but in a spot inconvenient to her, was upsetting. She disapproved of the height and unsightliness from her living room window. She concluded with, "Just because he's a cop he thinks he owns the world." I had mixed feelings about that neighbor for a long time.

Those of us married to an officer become a distinct group, kindred to the animal kingdom where the male travels for days searching for food for his family, fighting off predators and the elements of Mother Nature, while his mate quickly learns to protect her family from the uncertainty of the future. She learns to adapt to her environment alone, taking on the primary responsibility of caring for her young.

Even if I had known how demanding his job would be I still would have married him. After all, I was so hopelessly in love, what difference could his job make? It turned out to be a difficult year, but I met some wonderful friends who were in the same boat and we got together to share our thoughts, fears and ideas. We all agreed that we learned to become unselfish and that's a pretty good attribute to acquire, especially in this kind of society.

Sign Here

Once you and your spouse have made the decision that the police department will be a part of your future, the next step is the grueling procedure of applying. The package sent by the department is part of a lengthy process. The application itself is not extensive but there is a background check, personal assessment tests and interviews, all of which will take some time. Police services vary in their procedures. As of January 1999 the package for Toronto Police Service contains an Introduction Letter along with the fee structure, the Orientation and Pretest Guide, and the following forms: Prep Participation Information, Application Information, Applicant Registration, Application and Confidential Applicant Survey. (If you think this package of goodies will unnerve him, forget it. He'll go at it like a hungry bear.)

Quite a number of years ago when I applied to what was then known as the police force, I found myself sitting across from a tough boxer of a staff sergeant with a voice that barked out the questions like a string of orders. I sat upright filled with fear and the virtues and ambitions of a young man of 20 (with flame-colored hair). I thought the interview was going well until the sergeant asked, "Is it true what they say about people with red hair?"

"What's that?" I played along.

"You know," he growled sarcastically. "They lose their tempers, can't control themselves."

"No sir," I replied with an audible touch of my own sarcasm. "That's an old wives' tale."

He thanked me and I left feeling defeated. I was turned down a few weeks later and it took two years before I got the nerve to apply again. I still don't know whether I was turned down because of my red hair or because of my sarcasm.

The Applicant Information form provides a list of the "Essential Competencies" (knowledge, skills and abilities which a candidate must demonstrate before becoming a police officer). Under the heading of Self-Control the officer is told that he must have "the ability to keep your own emotions under control and to restrain negative actions when provoked or when working under a stressful situation." As police spouses we know very well what this statement really means:

1. You encounter a bank robber whose face is covered with a nylon stocking and toting a sawed off shotgun aimed straight for your head. Could you calmly ask him to drop his weapon and put his hands up?

2. A mother pushing her baby in a carriage walks across a busy city intersection and the carriage gets struck by a car. The buggy is lying in a mangled mess of spokes and canvas, baby

limbs and blood. Can you keep your composure long enough to quell the hysterics of that devastated mother?

3. A father and son are in a violent physical fight on the front lawn of their house. The neighbors have formed a circle around them. The eighteen-year-old son raises a jagged piece of glass from a broken bottle to his father's face, threatening to kill him. Can you speak calmly and sensibly to that hot-blooded young man, at the same time soothe the father and eliminate the heightening fear in the crowd?

4. A single mother of five is having difficulty making ends meet and has no moral or financial support from family and friends. She's at the breaking point and has been seen striking the children numerous times by different witnesses and has left the kids for long periods of time unattended. You, along with a social worker from the Children's Aid Society, have been appointed to take the children from their home. Could you pry a screaming child of two away from his mother, along with four brothers and sisters, and take them from the only home they've ever known?

Officers can and do deal with many difficult situations daily. The self-assessment is only a guide. (Do you think that this will deter him from applying now? Absolutely not! He'll be more determined to go out and save the world.)

Although it is not currently included, a Spousal Self-Assessment questionnaire is sorely needed to allow us a sneak preview of what lies ahead. Here are some questions that might be considered.

1. Are you prepared to deal with the demands that an officer's job will bring into the relationship?

2. Are you willing to put up with shifts, including evenings, nights, weekends, birthdays and special holidays?

3. Do you have the self-confidence to raise your family, knowing in advance that you cannot always have your spouse's total support?

4. Are you prepared to spend many evenings alone?

5. In the face of uncertainty, can you make quick decisions?

6. Are you able to deal with stressful situations in a calm and constructive way without blaming your spouse for choosing a profession with high demands?

7. Can you deal with the stress that an officer will bring home from work?

8. In most marriages there are many changes and you learn to grow with them, but in a police marriage are you willing to deal with a complete change of lifestyle?

For some of us the road will be tolerable due to certain personality traits of flexibility and resilience, but many of us will struggle to maintain a 'normal' sense of order only to find the changes will bring about depression, anger and futility. Don't despair—hundreds and thousands of us all over the world have been there and we understand.

The "Introduction to Policing" enclosed with the Toronto Police Service application package states:

A career in policing is primarily about one thing: working with people to ensure public safety through crime prevention and law enforcement. Police work requires that a constable be able to build relationships in the community, while showing sensitivity to and concern for the needs of people from all races, cultures and backgrounds.

The Police Services Act describes four key areas of responsibility for a police constable:

- preserving the peace
- preventing crimes and providing assistance to others in their prevention
- assisting victims of crime
- apprehending and charging offenders and executing warrants

In addition, a police officer is responsible for:
- referring individuals to community services and agencies
- educating the public

Police work is also demanding. A police constable must work shifts, including evenings, nights and weekends at all times of the year. This is not a job that everyone will like or can do well.

The last two sentences scream out a warning to the spouse as well as the applicant.

Training

Police college is an eventful experience for the new police recruit. Again, police departments vary in their training time. Toronto Police Service recruits begin at Bick College for a two-and-a-half-week orientation to service with an overview of technical skills and a chance to become accustomed to the language. From there they continue to the Ontario Police College in Aylmer, Ontario, for 12 weeks, where they perform basic recruit training, or foundation training. This time away from home is when you learn the meaning of 'absence makes the heart grow fonder'. When that exhausting stretch of work is over he returns to Bick College for eight more weeks for the Urban Community Policing course, where he will complete his education with specific and expanded training, participate in live scenarios and attend a ride-along with a senior officer. In spite of this intensive training, officers still learn the majority of their skills on the street and from veteran officers.

Sergeant Lynn Taylor, instructor for Bick College in Scarborough, Ontario, becomes very attached to her new recruits, sharing in their accomplishments and reassuring them when times get tough. In a telephone interview, she related:

*I try to encourage a balance of lifestyle and reinforce the neces-
sity to take care of their emotional and physical well-being. They
begin to realize that they are radically different and are considered as a police culture or a part of 'the blue wall'. I repeatedly communicate to them the importance of remembering the support and strength they receive from family and friends and to
never lose sight of that.*

Sergeant Taylor has experienced the frustrations that lie ahead of
these new recruits and she helps to guide them with strength, energy
and compassion.

When a constable is finished training he (or she) is expected to be
the model police officer who will be able to make sound judgments,
take charge of crisis situations and handle calls with common sense
and courage. There is an amazing metamorphosis that takes place
when that new rookie leaves for work those first few weeks in his
newly pressed uniform, spit-polished boots and gleaming hat badge.
He becomes a proud, self-respecting, sturdy and reliable example of
the good values of our society. He is ready to fight the world single-
handedly. This will also be a frustrating time for a new officer as he
finds he is the joe being sent to the small menial calls of neighborhood complaints, false alarms, noise disturbances and minor violations. He becomes the 'yes man' in the office, trying desperately to
please his superiors. Meanwhile, the senior officers are having a little fun with him.

Those first weeks are also the time when you will find you are both
feeling a little bewildered, rocking back and forth, looking for some
common ground. You have endured your spouse's endless nights
away at police college, you have been thrown into the chaotic shift-
work schedule that brings about disorganization, confusion and
aggravation, and you have this dark foreboding that things are never
going to get better. But be assured that they do! Take a really good

look at your spouse. Have you ever seen him look so splendid and happy? He is so caught up in police work that he is now providing you with every minute detail of each call, often with brutally vivid descriptions. Your childish naïveté toward police work eggs him on, so that you can soon recite all the city laws and police procedures.

If you are completely honest with yourself you will admit that this is a very exciting time. Your relationship is filled with new experiences and a powerful communication that is invigorating (not to mention how you feel every time you see him in uniform). Just let yourself relax and you will ride the roller coaster of a whole new and electrifying world.

The time will eventually come when all that enthusiasm comes crashing to a stop, but that too is only for a short while. Each crisis call that the officer attends will deflate him until he learns to deal with his feelings and becomes more and more competent. These calls build stamina and character, shaping him into a model police officer. You will never be as proud of him as you are right now!

A wife from the Buffalo Police Department remembers her husband's first three weeks on the job:

We had been married for four years before Jackson got on the police department and you'd never believe the change in him. He whistled all the time, he walked with his head up high and he had a self-confidence I'd never seen in him before. He felt good about himself 'cause he loved what he was doing. It was the only time I remember him being really happy since I'd met him. I even found myself defending the honor of every cop in the city.

What About Us?

There is no college or special training for police spouses to teach us how to deal with what lies ahead. As with parenting skills, there are no physical or mental assessments to allow us to determine whether we are qualified. We, too, will learn our new skills on the job.

Very few departments offer seminars for the spouse of an officer. The ones that do provide that option find that many spouses have good intentions but never find the time to attend. Let me stress the importance of these seminars, if only for the support and the connections with other spouses that they provide. Each department should strive to make these seminars mandatory for spouses, partners, parents and children of graduating officers. Each person should also be given the opportunity to join a staff sergeant on a ride-along so that they can obtain first-hand experience in police work.

I wish I'd married him after he'd been on the department for a while. I think that would have given him time to become more accustomed to the work load and maybe pacify his more untamed nature. Maybe then it would finally have gone out of his system and he would have been more prepared to cope with the responsibilities of a relationship and a family.

In fact, the job will always hold the same basic excitement, challenges and fears for the officer. One spouse remarked that police families are not the only ones where the spouse's profession is demanding and challenging. His wife is the president of a large financial institution.

She's never home. She flies all over the country while the kids and I are left to fend for ourselves. I performed all the duties that I thought she was supposed to do. I really resented her job those first few years but she brought in the bigger dollar. Over time I became a master chef and a darn good father.

Not all applicants survive police college and some never make it through their first year on the road, either because they are not suited for the job, or because they lack the mental and physical skills required. For those who become police officers it's still not known whether they choose the job or the job chooses them. But once they become a cop, there is no escape.

Below is a letter written by a police officer to his spouse:

Someone asked me the other day if I still loved my job and my immediate response was "Of course!" Then he asked me if you liked it and with uncertainty I responded "I guess so." It was the first time anyone had asked me that question and it prompted me to look back through my career and I recalled some pretty tough times.

Remember when you stayed up with me all night because I had been to my first suicide and I couldn't shake the memory of that poor 35-year-old mother hanging from the maple tree in her backyard, her tongue long and black and her eyes rolled back into her head, her 10-year-old son begging, "Mamma, wake up, pleeease." Did I thank you for listening, for being there to share my tears?

How could I forget the night the neighbor rushed you to the hospital to give birth to our first child. I was on midnights and had to guard a murder scene. I wasn't there when your water broke and the cramps gripped your stomach like mammoth monster claws and you cried out for me in the delivery room. I arrived just in time to hear our baby's first cry. Did I tell you I was sorry for not being there for you when you needed me most and thank you for giving me the most precious gifts in the world, our son and your unconditional love?

Remember the day I called you from the hospital because some drug addict pulled a knife on me, slashing my arm in his attempt to get away? I told you I only required a few stitches and that I'd be O.K. but you rushed to emergency to sit by me, hiding your nervousness with that silly crooked smile of yours and your hand over mine. You drove me home, administered my pain killers, tucked me into bed and crawled in gently beside me. Did I tell you how much I appreciated your loyalty and all your small unselfish acts of love?

Thanks for being intuitive enough to know when I needed my space on those 'bad' days and when to be open enough to listen to the rendition of calls that would make even the toughest of men sick to their stomachs. I want to tell you that you are the most important person in my life and without you nothing else matters. I love you more than you will ever know.

So when I finally had the nerve to ask you how you liked being married to a cop I should have known what your reply would be.

"I'm so proud of you," you simply stated.

What more could I ask for?

In the survey, I asked the question, "If you ever had to remarry would you marry another cop?" Surprisingly, 85 percent said yes and 10 percent said they already had. All of them admitted that once you got used to the lifestyle you would never go back.

If as a police spouse you find at any time that you feel confused, fearful or uncertain in any way about your new lifestyle, call and ask any police department for literature, reference materials or seminars that they might provide. There is very little material written for the spouse of an officer but there is help. By seeking the support of family, friends and other police spouses or joining organizations such as the Police Spouse Association or calling the Employee Assistance Program, you will find assistance is not far away.

There is an urgent need to educate officers and their families about the joys and pitfalls of this kind of marriage. For the new spouses of police officers this book will provide some insight as to what you can expect in your new lifestyle, and for those who have been in a police marriage for some time, this book will allow you to feel that you are not alone during the more turbulent times and will hopefully provide a positive outlook. In the meantime, we will all proudly continue to wear the invisible badge.

Love That Uniform

You cannot win in every situation,
you cannot keep all teardrops in your eye.
Remember through the anger and frustration,
this world's a better place because you try.
And so if these reflections that you ponder
can help you find a balanced point of view,
the day will come when once again I'll see you
stand straight and tall and proud—to wear the blue.

from "Wearing the Blue"
Terry McGarry © 1994

I fell in love with my first uniformed man at the age of seven. His name was Joseph Morellos and we called him Little Joe for short. He was older, at least nine. His buzzed blond hair was invariably covered with a honey-colored straw cowboy hat, trimmed in dark brown vinyl. A piercing silver whistle hung from its twisted blue and white ties. Under the brim were the squinted eyes of a true crime-fighting sheriff, knife-like blue and glowering. His freckled right hand was never far from the engraved silver six-gun which was lodged in the sleeve of a very fine tan holster that hung lopsided just below his right knee. Little of the red paint on that silver star that pronounced "Sheriff" was still decipherable, but Little Joe polished that metal until it blinded our young eyes.

Little Joe's purposeful swagger and slow drawl made my knees weak and my stomach lurch high up into my throat as if I were on a Ferris wheel. He protected me from the 'bad guys'; he was my hero.

What is it about a person in uniform? What makes them so sexy, so respected and feared? I admit that I have a passion for uniforms. I can't help myself. From airline captains to hockey players, from our military boys to our doctors, I become weak and silly, but there are none as intriguing as that of a police officer. The thick dark blue cotton pants with the bright red stripe that falls orderly and unruffled over polished black boots. The dark multi-pocketed shirt stretches over the armor, accentuating large chests with epaulets implying wide shoulders. The thick black leather belt suspended from the waist holds the dangerous tools of their trade, inspiring mystery and fear. The forage cap with a patent brim adds exaggerated height and formality, while the shiny badge and cool eyes represent authority. The combination evokes some pretty powerful feelings. Even after 20 years of marriage I still become helpless to that volcanic rush I feel each time I see Paul in uniform. I can always count on it!

One officer's wife, with a deep sigh, remembers:

I attended a police function. Everywhere I looked there were police officers in full uniform from departments all around the world. The air was filled with a unexplainable electricity. It was an awesome feeling.

Dicken's *Pickwick Papers* (1837) said it best: "A good uniform must work its way with the women, sooner or later."

A Powerful Effect

A police uniform is a strong symbol of power, effectiveness, security, strength and authority. The public understands that a uniformed officer is there to enforce the law and there is never any mistaking who he is. An officer knows that when he dons the uniform and goes to work he must provide the very best example he can and nothing less. He maintains law and order simply by wearing the uniform. That in itself can be stressful to an officer. The uniform carries a stereotype of authority that can assist or burden him.

Paul remembers sitting in a café waiting for his partner. It was a busy working day with a long line-up of customers waiting for their coffee and sandwiches. The customers kept looking in his direction, some stares being more obvious then others. Paul became increasingly uncomfortable until he was finally forced to go and stand outside. When he rose, the room became totally silent and a long line-up of heads followed him out.

"I'm used to people staring but I guess sometimes it just gets to you," he remarked. "What I find really annoying is when you're hungry and grab something on the run and people slow down to look into the police car to see what you're doing and what you're eating. Wearing a uniform comes with a price. You never really have any privacy." Paul loved his childhood, when kids would pretend they were the good guy wearing the blue. "Now," he shakes his head, "kids fight over who wants to be the bad guy. Times have really changed."

Members of the family, friends and neighbors may directly feel the impact that the uniform has. Talking to someone you love dressed in jeans feels different from talking to him when he's dressed in uniform. Initial reactions can range from trust and respect, to a feeling of distance, to negative feelings such as fear. Some people are not affected. Dan's father remembers:

For the longest time I felt really uncomfortable around Dan when he came home in uniform. I'd always been the disciplinarian in our house and Dan was the most difficult of our four children. When he was dressed for work I felt different around him, more reserved. I wasn't sure where I stood any longer until one evening when Dan returned from work after a teen suicide call. I found him slumped over the table, his hat beside him and his head in his hands. I realized he needed me just as much now but in a different way. I was still his father but also his friend.

It's in fact what the uniform represents that draws the attention—belonging to an old institution with a solid and reliable foundation that can be trusted, one that has been a part of our history for centuries. Two hundred years ago there were no uniforms; officers were called watchmen and were conscripted by the government to perform police duties without pay. An appointed watchman could relieve himself from these duties by paying a sum of 25 dollars. This was a job no one wanted until 1834, when the government finally offered a small salary.

Uniform History

The uniform itself has not changed much in the last hundred years. It was designed to differentiate police officers from other uniformed workers, such as the milkman, gas attendant, sales representative, delivery person and military. In Canada and some states in the United States they were modeled after Britain's bobby. Changes were made to the original uniform thanks to the public, who felt sorry for police officers in discomfort. Some public-spirited citizens approached politicians to allow police officers to seek more comfortable dress so that they could do their job more efficiently.

The uniform of 1860-1946 was the box neck tunic and the bobby-style helmet. Next came the open-neck tunics with collar and tie and the forage cap. Now the officer is more comfortable with a simple lightweight shirt, although he must wear, as always, a cumbersome bullet-proof vest. In winter when jackets are worn a tie is required, but in the hot summer months there is no tie and the collar may remain open.

There was a time when officers were expected to pay for some parts of their uniform, such as white gloves for special occasions. In those years the officer's baton was held in a scabbard. Next came the 12-inch wood sticks with a leather grab strap attached that slipped into the pocket. Now, depending on whether the officer is on a bike, car, motorcycle or on the beat, he may carry a plastic baton or a steel collapsible asp.

The uniforms have always resembled the quasi-military and para-military because of the need to use force. There is also a similarity in the strict discipline of dress. All police officers are turned out to look the same. An officer is expected to be tidy and neat, with hair cut and boots clean. This type of dress code helps to instill confidence in the public.

When my husband started in the department over twenty years ago he told me he was shown how to clean his boots by 'spit and polish'. I thought he was joking but every night after dinner he laid some newspaper down on the kitchen floor and picking up one at a time, he spat on the toe of the leather boot. Then, rubbing in small clockwise circles with a soft cloth, he waxed them until they mirrored his satisfied gaze. You've never seen anything so shiny in your life. You'd think they were black patent leather. With the new kinds of polish and buffers available, officers no longer need to use the old technique, but there are not many boots out there that are as quite as nice as they were with the 'spit and polish' ritual.

Each police department around the world and each unit within the department, from tactical and undercover to administrative and drug squad, has its own dress code for recognition, confidentiality and comfort.

An Important Part of Society

Officers feel a sense of power when wearing a uniform. It's part and parcel of upholding the law, of putting their life on the line, and being able to take charge of any situation. Often the uniform becomes a second skin, a way of life, and the change back to civilian clothing can be traumatic, because it no longer commands a response from the public. Officers who were once in uniform and changed to civilian clothing, or those who have retired, have difficulty adjusting to the 'normal' lifestyle.

Bert's last position in the department was as a safety officer, traveling to the different schools in the area and talking to teachers and classrooms. He was very proud of being a police officer and knew nothing else. Wearing a uniform identified him as a very important part of our society. When he finished his last day at the station, he said goodbye to his friends with promises of getting together and he set his badge and gun on the desk for the last time. That was so hard for him, but what was more critical was hanging up his uniform for good. He had it cleaned and it hung in the spare room closet for good. Sometimes I'd hear him opening the door to sneak a peek and sometimes I'd catch him feeling the material. Once he tried on the tunic and with an embarrassed laugh told me that he just wondered if it still fit.

Wearing a police uniform brings about a personality switch. Some psychologists who have studied uniforms and their impact remark that it carries very high morals and standards to the workplace. Unfortunately, in some cases it also brings those that abuse the uniform and use it to elevate their egos by increasing their personal power.

One husband, whose experience married to a police officer was a difficult one, recalls:

She changed a lot when she put on that uniform. She has a tiny frame but boy, she developed this BIG personality. With time she became more and more like an officer and less and less like a civilian, until she completely lost her identity. She always talked down to me. It got to the point where she dominated and commanded our relationship. We ended up seeking counseling before things got to a stage where they were irreparable.

Fortunately the majority of officers are more than happy to keep their home as a safe and relaxing haven and are willing to join their families in a comfortable atmosphere away from work. But the family does have to expect definite changes in the officer's personality when he dons the uniform.

Marianne, the wife of a Royal Canadian Mounted Police officer, observed:

It was as if he was a Jekyll and Hyde. One minute he was like every father on the block, chasing the kids on his hands and knees all around the kitchen table until they pleaded for mercy, and the next minute he was dressed for work and unapproachable, carrying that cool and distant disposition they all seem to have. The kids never really understood it and I had a hard time, but I respected it just the same. I guess they use the uniform to toughen their skins so that they can handle what's out there.

Officers cannot be seen kissing and hugging in public. They must maintain a professional image at all times. The rules have become a little more relaxed recently, so that they can be more approachable to the public.

Last summer John was stationed at a summer amusement park. I decided I'd take the girls for the rides and to see their dad at work. It's a funny feeling when you're walking toward your husband in a public place while he's working. Really weird, kind of like walking toward a stranger that you happen to know everything about. The kids ran to him without the inhibitions and intuition of an adult and threw themselves around his legs, hugging. Mary lifted her arms to be picked up and instead of reaching down for her, John gently patted her blond curls and took hold of her hand so that he could walk us to the next ride. He watched us from a distance and his huge smile was unmistakable. I could tell he would have loved to jump on the merry-go-round with them. I kind of felt sorry for him.

Comfort and Safety

Wearing a uniform changes the way police officers feel, walk and talk. They fit into what is called a "survival mindset" that allows them to carry out their duties. The additional clothing adds bulk and height and the silver buttons, bands and badges command recognition. The dark blue has always been a fashionable traditional color that remains conservative and sophisticated and doesn't show the ravages of the weather, the grime and blood. Many police services are experimenting with a new issue of a black uniform. The contemplated change involves safety issues, where the dark color will ensure safety in the evening.

Officers are looking for uniforms that are safe and comfortable. Changes will reflect their likes and dislikes. The need for dark colors, lightweight materials, nylon belts and light body armor, velcro pockets, sturdy lightweight running shoes and repellent jackets will allow them to perform with less restraint and more comfort. Many materials are washable and many departments offer dry cleaning vouchers to help maintain a professional image.

The body armor is the most important part of the uniform. Officers can now wear it over their shirts to prevent irritation and sweating. The armor is made of a woven ballistic fabric and non-woven reinforced plastic. At first officers made excuses that they were too uncomfortable and it made them look fat. Furthermore, it invaded their 'macho' image and consequently they adopted the 'it won't happen to me' attitude. Fortunately the vest has been made mandatory and has saved many officers from being killed. It is not yet as flexible nor as breathable and light as they would like, but newer materials are always being tested. Merely wearing the body armor can sometimes be enough to deter negative action from criminals by enforcing the 'ready for action' appearance.

Officers also have a distinct walk that secures an immediate calming effect on citizens. It is slow and deliberate but with a definite purpose. A police officer who is about to give out a ticket will often put on his hat, slowly open his door to step out, adjust his coat and with caution traverse the length of the two cars unhurried, standing cautiously behind the driver's window.

A jumpy, reckless police officer who bolts toward a driver may cause the driver distress and put his own life in danger. The walk is intentionally defensive and controlled for protection.

I remember when Amy slipped on some stones in the little river that ran through our backyard. She screamed for help and Todd, who was sitting beside me, got up seemingly unperturbed and slowly walked toward the river, assuring Amy that he was close and would help her and just to relax. If I could have moved out of my frozen state I think I would have picked up the lawn chair and thrown it directly at his head to wake him up. Only after he carefully lifted Amy out of the water and checked to make sure she hadn't broken anything did I notice his face was drawn and pale.

A police officer's comforting movements and voice have saved people from being hurt and killed. They impart reassurance and security to those who are distraught. Uniformed officers learn how to approach people to make them feel comfortable and safe. The uniform acts as an icebreaker for citizens who need a strong shoulder. The subtle air of responsibility and authority commands respect.

An officer's speech is usually enunciated from the front of the mouth to sound authoritative and the voice deepens and becomes more stern. Depending on the situation, a stone-cold, reserved facial expression can make citizens feel they are unapproachable and impartial. This too is for the officer's protection. Everything about an officer demands attention and shows he is in control and ready to respond at all times.

Our family and Paul's brother and his family had gone camping a number of years ago. At 2:00 a.m. our son Trevor fell out of his bunk and called out with an unusual cry. I awoke in shock, struggling to get out of my sleeping bag to help him. The darkness and strangeness confused me and I passed out, something I had never done in my life. Paul heard the thud when my head hit the floor and called out to his brother for help. They lifted me to the bed and gently shook me. When I came to he asked me some questions and I went limp in his arms, passing out again. When I finally regained consciousness I saw a terrible fear in Paul's eyes. He admits it was the first time he felt so out of control. It's different when it's a stranger, but when it's your own family you feel helpless.

Children love to see their parents in uniform. Their friends ask in awe, "Wow, is your mom a cop? That's so wicked!" They are proud of their officer parent and the response the uniform brings. As children mature, they must deal with comments from friends that are not always positive and may prefer not to disclose their parent's occupation, but they never lose that sense of pride.

Paul has a trick that has become a family joke. When our children, Michelle and Trevor, invite new friends over, he strategically places his police hat or shirt where it can be seen. For years it went unnoticed by both kids because they were so used to seeing them around, but they've since become wise. Just a little reminder to enjoy some good clean fun.

The kids love to dress up in Trisha's uniform. They would fight over who would wear the hat. Her heavy jacket would hang down past their ankles, slipping off their shoulders, and the hat sat precariously on their little heads and tilted to one side. They marched around the room with great seriousness or hid behind the couch and re-enacted a detective scene from television, shouting "stick 'em up!" The kids are in their twenties now but even though they get great pleasure out of teasing their mom in her 'dress-up' clothes, they still have a great amount of respect for the job she does.

How Bad Can It Be?

Paul has recently expressed some distress over wearing his uniform, especially since he's reached his forties and put on a little weight. He complains bitterly that it's too heavy for running in, too tight, and the vest is too hot and too constricting. I have often remarked that he should stop complaining, after all he's worn it for over 20 years. His answer has always been the same: "Why don't you try it for 10 hours a day and see how it feels?"

So to appease him and for the benefit of myself and the readers I decided I might as well get the full appreciation of how he feels. The effect was not just a physical strain but a physiological one as well. The false appearance that an officer in full uniform looks comfortable and natural didn't take long to be squelched after my "day in uniform."

First I decided to weigh myself and then get into full dress and weigh myself again. It was only about 20 pounds extra. Having been pregnant twice, this would be a breeze.

I laid out the full uniform and gear, consisting of the parka, shirt with epaulets, hat, boots, body armor, pants, pant belt, leather police belt containing miter, pepper spray, handcuffs, rubber glove pouch, ammunition pouch and ammunition, holster and unloaded gun, billy, small flashlight, badge, small notebook and pen. Our queen-size bed was covered with the severe colors of clothing, metal and leather.

I began with the shirt and epaulets. It felt crisp, light, and I looked pretty cool. Next came the pants and belt. Not bad at all. Then I strapped on the gun belt over the pant belt, with all the tools attached. Paul helped me tighten it so that it fit snugly around my waist. Now that was a little more uncomfortable; as a matter of fact, the belt crushed my intestines and my rib cage and I felt as if two giant hands were pushing down on my hips. I noticed in the mirror that I had suddenly developed a squared-off butt and ample hippo hips. Okay, definitely not flattering. Now I understood the comment from one police officer married to another:

I don't really find it particularly attractive on her. I prefer to see her in a skirt or jeans. Actually I'd rather see her in anything but her uniform.

I slipped on the size eleven boots—a little like wearing Daddy's but at least comfortable. I wiggled my big toes until I could feel the leather, softly rippled from miles of walking on pavement. I began to notice that objects were needling me, pointed, rounded, pushing and poking into my waist and my hips and scratching at my shoulders and legs. I tried to readjust a few but they had found their snug space and refused to move. I was beginning to feel a new kind of anxiety.

The vest was the one article of clothing I was most concerned about because of Paul's constant complaints about its being burdensome and heavy. Well, he was right. It pulled down on my shoulders as if a gymnast were performing on top of them. I developed an immediate flat chest and instant muscles. No wonder officers looked intimidating. I stood in front of the mirror with my legs apart and my hand on the billy. I looked like I meant business. I fancied myself talking to a person or two that had done me harm in years past.

"Licence, ownership and insurance," I bellowed in the deepest throaty voice I could muster. "Terry," I said out loud, reading the licence. "I remember you. Terry Teaser from grade 2. Aren't you the one that hid one of my snow boots in the bathroom garbage?" I entertained myself for a few minutes, finding it a cathartic exercise, but it was a physiologically dangerous walk to take. I felt as if I could rule the world single-handedly, that I was infallible. I wanted to shout out orders and run out to save the world.

I lifted the heavy parka off the bed, a big sheet of padded vinyl with a quilted liner to keep you warm. Now that was really complimentary. I now resembled a refrigerator.

Last and least flattering was the hat. Perched on the top of my head it forced my chin-length curly black hair out from under the brim like a clown's. How could anyone take me seriously? The hat was heavy and just tight enough to cause a deep purple ridge across my forehead and the beginning of a splitting headache. The small knife-like pin that holds the badge to the front of the hat protruded inwards. If you were ever pushed into something or hit on that spot you would instantly inherit a hole deep into the skull bone.

Pregnancy was beginning to be remembered as wonderful. I began to feel more like a prisoner then a police officer. Paul sat on the edge of the bed with a smug smile. "Wow," he remarked. "It fits."

Thanks, that's just what I wanted to hear from my husband. I was determined to show him that I was not in the least uncomfortable.

I continued my regular routine, plugging in the kettle, putting away a few dishes, pouring my tea and heading up to the office. I made it up the first five stairs and had to stop. With each step things dug into me from all sides and the added weight was tiresome. I made it to the top of the flight of 16 steps, panting. Paul slowly followed behind me pushing out a slow whistle. "Watch it," I huffed. "I've got the stick."

I placed the cup on my desk, pulled my chair up in front of the computer and tried to sit down. I couldn't bend. I had to let myself fall back into the chair, almost flipping myself over.

I gripped the desk and steadied myself to bring me back upright. I heard a snicker at the doorway. At this stage I knew I couldn't run for him; instead I gave him that hard cold stare that officers are so good at, and it worked. I don't think it was the uniform, though.

I didn't sit for long. I was too conscious of my headache and the beginning of a stomach ache. Sitting for a long period of time would probably not be a good idea. I pulled myself up out of the chair and walked back down the stairs. A much easier procedure. I wondered how officers managed to chase their suspects through trees, over fences and around buildings without suffering exhaustion or near heart failure, laden with such a load.

I was into the second month of my new job on the police department when I developed a constant searing pain in my right shoulder. I worked as a cadet before the department and was used to wearing a uniform so I would never have guessed the problem. I saw the doctor, who concluded it must be the addition of the gun. Sure enough, my shoulder was compensating for the extra weight.

I made my way to the backyard, walking the turf as opposed to walking the beat. I began by marching in a one-two-three step, then bending, walking quickly, running around the birch tree, jumping over the pond and finally taking the one-kneed shooting position, panting and perspiring. I couldn't have shot the back fence if I'd tried.

The last attempt at police exercise was to jam myself into our medium-sized car. I had predicted it would be awkward. The problem was not in getting into the car, which I did by carefully sliding in sideways and pushing the small of my back into the seat, but in getting out of the car. It was impossible. The butt of the gun caught the steering wheel and hooked me like an anchor caught in a jagged piece of rock. I wasn't going anywhere. I leaned back, placing my foot on the ground, and by grasping the steering wheel and turning myself so that I was going out backside first, I managed to swing back around and land on the ground feet first. In the process I dropped my pen. Realizing that bending was not going to be an easy feat, I used the exercise that people with bad backs practice, bending at the knees and retrieving the item without falling face first into the asphalt.

This maneuver did not go unnoticed. A very supportive friend decided to drop by for a quick unexpected visit. She had just arrived home from a wonderful holiday in Mexico and wanted to model her braided and beaded hair. I didn't see her but I heard her heroic struggle to choke down the beginning of convulsive laughter. What could I do but invite her in?

This mode of dress was not for entertaining, and it gave me the reprieve I was looking for. I slipped thankfully into my comfortable jeans and T-shirt, returning to my normal existence without a second glance. Those three and a half hours had seemed an eternity. It wasn't just the awkwardness of the clothing but the weighty responsibility that I had felt the minute the uniform was in place.

Paul walked by. "Done already?" he asked. "Donna just dropped in," I replied weakly.

He was kind enough to let it be.

Next Shift!

Shift work can cause a multitude of problems in a police family. Studies have proven the divorce rate is much higher than in other families due to relationships becoming strained adjusting to this lifestyle. The officer has a higher risk of developing physical problems because of poor eating habits and sleep deprivation. These families can learn to adjust to this irregular and erratic lifestyle by making positive changes that will allow them a greater sense of flexibility, self-worth and in turn draws a family closer together.

The alarm shrieked so loudly that it began an angry march across the beside table. Paul administered a little cuff at the unnerving sound, and we sleepily acknowledged its noisy tumble to the floor. Then silence. That was our cue, our Monday to Friday ritual. Weekends were sacred. Friday was wind-down night with a movie, Saturday we grocery shopped, cleaned our little apartment and partied. Sunday was our very favourite, untroubled day. This wonderfully 'normal' and consistent lifestyle was soon to change into a nightmare of shift work.

Paul's first week of police work in March of 1980 was a midnight shift. I had evolved from a home where I'd spent the first seven years of my life sleeping in my womb-like bed beside my parents, the next 13 in the room next door, and then moved from the old nest to the new one with Paul. I had never spent a night alone. That first week was a week from hell. I couldn't sleep. There was no amount of television, reading or exercise that would allow me the pleasure of sweet slumber. On the third or fourth night I sat on our endlessly vast queen-size bed angrily plucking lint from Paul's old hunting sweater cursing, "I love you, I love you NOT!"

I called my mother and told her I was moving back into my old room. She was sympathetic but insisted that I had no choice but to get used to being alone. I married him and I had made a commitment. By the end of the sixth month, I was a nervous wreck and I wanted out of this 'commitment'. I was ready to pack it in.

The only thing shift work can be likened to is caring for an infant—a constant disruption of work and sleep to tend to feedings, diaper changes and cranky teething. As in parenting, police spouses never have the luxury of a regular solid sleep pattern. When the officer arrives home at the end of a 4:00 a.m. shift, as quiet as he thinks he may be, the officer's spouse will undoubtedly awaken. Some spouses are awake long enough to mumble some inaudible night-time garble, some toss and turn until the sandman comes once again, while others lie awake the rest of the night beside their snoring mate.

Rob came home from a stressful evening shift where a young teenage girl had tried to commit suicide by slashing her wrists. The quick thinking of a neighbor and help from police and ambulance saved the girl's life, but it was the bloody scene that confronted Rob when he arrived that horrified him. That night he roamed throughout the house, alternately opening the pantry doors and the refrigerator. I heard him talking to himself, and sighing, and then the clink of the beer cap hitting the side of the stainless steel sink and spinning to a stop. Next was the television and another clink. At that point I couldn't get back to sleep anyway so I thought I'd try to convince him to come to bed. He kept saying he wasn't tired and I knew this was going to be another one of 'those' nights. He would never admit it, but he needed to talk. Before I knew it, the sun had crept up over the back fence and it was time for me to get ready for work.

This is not an uncommon occurrence in a police family. Spouses and children are affected by the officer's shifts in every way. They deal with the never-ending shift rotation, the calendar planning, diet change and irregular sleep patterns. "Some workers can get pulled into a negative, self-perpetuating cycle of poor family life, poor job performance, and poor health. This destructive cycle can ultimately lead to lowered self-esteem, depression, divorce, and job loss." (From *Working the Shift* by C. Shapiro, M.D., R. Heslegrave, Joanne Beyers and L. Picard.) The first year is the most difficult to adjust to, but with smart planning and a strict schedule, shift work will become bearable. The spouse must be willing to make sacrifices.

Shift Work Schedules

There are many variables to a shift depending on the police department. Below is a typical Toronto Police shift, which may vary depending on which platoon the officer is assigned to. Generally with uniformed officers there are three basic shifts—days, afternoons and midnights. Each shift lasts seven days. The hours of these shifts may fluctuate by one hour at the beginning and the end depending upon how the platoon is split. This provides an overlap of uniformed officers, those ending the midnight shift and others who are beginning the day shift, allowing for continual police coverage at all times. Formats may differ from division to division.

Day Shift

    Start: 6:30-7:30 a.m.

    End: 4:30-5:30 p.m.

    Equaling 10 hours 6 days off

Afternoon Shift
    Start: 4:00-5:00 p.m.
    End: 2:00-3:00 a.m.
    Equaling 10 hours 5 days off
Midnights
    Start: 11:00 p.m-2:00 a.m.
    End: 7:00-8:00 a.m.
    Equaling 8 hours 3 days off

Generally in the course of an officer's day he is allowed a one-hour lunch break. Quite often in the busier divisions there is no time for lunch and the officer can bank his hour or go home one hour early. In small towns officers and military police are often called upon for their services during their time off.

In the survey conducted, 70 percent of the police officers disliked day shift most, and 90 percent of the spouses agreed that midnight shift was the most difficult, followed by afternoons.

The Effects of Shift Work

The mortality rate of an officer is higher than in any other occupation. Officers who have insufficient sleep will feel lethargic, moody, frustrated, irritable and possibly depressed, and will have difficulty concentrating. They may experience physical symptoms of body fatigue, stomach upsets and headaches. One officer who has been on the police department for 30 years remarked, "I find shift work gets harder as you get older. Once you get to your mid-thirties you start to notice that time seems to go by too quickly. Shift work really takes its toll on you."

Getting quality sleep is the single most important factor of shift work. By understanding what happens to the body during a normal cycle we can better understand the complexities that arise from an irregular shift pattern. When an officer doesn't feel 'normal' or is feeling 'dragged out' it's imperative that he understand there is a logical medical reason for it. A handbook put out by the Porcupine Health Unit and Sudbury District Health Unit called "Shift Work Like Clockwork," dated March 1995, states:

> Our built-in clock ticks on a 24-hour schedule, controlling sleep, play, rest and work. This amazing clock also controls body temperature, pulse, blood pressure, kidney function, hormone production, digestion, etc. The built-in clock is called our CIRCADIAN CYCLE ("circa" means "about" and "dias" means "day"). Humans function best during the daytime and sleep best at night.
>
> Temperature rises before we get up and stays up during daytime hours. We are functioning at peak efficiency—alert, digestion is working and physical strength is "high" then...temperature drops at night along with blood pressure, pulse, digestion, etc. At this time, we are less alert, strength is decreased and the ability to think and make decisions is impaired.
>
> For mind and body to work well, our built-in clock must tick on a regular schedule. We use cues like day and night, mealtimes and activities to set the clock.
>
> With a regular 24-hour clock, the period of alertness and least urge to sleep is mid-morning and early evening. The strongest feelings to sleep are from 3 to 6 a.m., and in the mid-afternoon, which is called "the post lunch dip."
>
> When a person works rotating shifts, the clock is out of sync. It means going home after nights to sleep, but the body and its systems are waking up. Feeling out of sync can lead to chronic fatigue, feelings of being run down and depression. The good news is that lifestyle changes make a person feel better and enjoy life more.

Lack of sleep can cause serious consequences to an officer's health and sense of well-being. The family must work together in maintaining a quiet and restful atmosphere for the officer to live in so that he can be allowed the maximum amount of restoration time.

At work, the officer may find his level of efficiency is dramatically affected. He may be unable to stay awake through the course of the evening. He may find he is fatigued and lacks physical strength. He may also notice he experiences a slower response time to a call or possibly doesn't even hear the call come through the radio. Upon proceeding to a high-stress call the officer may feel he is reacting to a situation in slow motion and is unprepared to protect himself or the public, which could cause himself or others unnecessary injuries. This lack of proficiency can make him irritable and impatient with the public, resulting in a higher number of complaints against him. Although sleep and relaxation are the simplest solution to some of these problems, an officer must recognize the problem first. Officers who do not recognize the problems that lack of sleep can cause may become dependent on caffeine to stay awake, alcohol to get to sleep or prescription and over-the-counter drugs.

The rate of sick days will increase if there is inability to function due to improper sleep and fatigue. The drive home from work, when the officer is finally allowed the luxury of winding down, is the most dangerous. He can become drowsy and unfocused, resulting in injury or death. Officers have double the chances of being killed during midnights than on a daytime shift.

A news item from the *CPA Express*, a Canadian police magazine, states: "DIED: Michel Leblanc, 21, a constable with the Assomption, Que. Police Service, early Dec. 31 after his car slammed into a parked truck on a highway near Montreal. Leblanc had just finished his overnight policing shift, followed by four hours of volunteer work…when he fell asleep at the wheel of his car while on his way home."

Many stations have a quiet room with a cot for those officers who need to catch some sleep after a night shift and before court or a paid duty. An officer should recognize exhaustion before getting into his vehicle to drive home. If he should become sleepy while driving he should pull over to a safe spot off the road, lock the doors and rest for 20 minutes or half an hour until he feels refreshed, or walk briskly around the car a few times, stretch all the limbs, take a few deep breaths and try again. Car pooling might be a solution for afternoons and midnights.

I remember the times when I'd be up through the night with babies for feedings or cranky teething. I would call Mike on the cell phone when I knew his shift was over and talk. This way I could keep us both awake. If the baby was still awake when he arrived, he would take over the rocking or walking and let me get back to sleep. He found this more therapeutic than unwinding in front of the television.

If you happen to be driving on a highway at 4:00 a.m. and observe a glassy-eyed driver go by with the windows wide open in the dead of winter and the radio blaring a pretty mean beat, you can bet it's some poor officer trying desperately to keep awake. Give him a cheerful wave to encourage his safe trip home.

At home, a chronically tired officer will have difficulty devoting quality time to his family. He may become moody, lack patience and have trouble focusing.

What Can You Do?

As the spouse of an officer, be alert to symptoms such as a lack of communication, irritability, quick temper, lethargy, overuse of drugs or alcohol or a change in personality.

In a police family bedtime could be any time of the day or night. By following some easy steps you can help your spouse sleep more readily and soundly. Begin by keeping the room dark, by providing curtains that have an added blackout lining. This gives the officer the sensation that it is night.

Last year I decided that our room needed a fresh new look. I impulsively purchased a dramatic chaise lounge in large fuscia and cherry-red roses and brilliant yellow daylilies. It had been unusually cold that winter and I longed for the amorous warmth of spring and the long curled green fingers of my tulip leaves. I made the decision to paint our room a soft butter yellow.

Paul had a few days off and began the preparations. As usual, I had the task of painting trim, carrying the ladder and passing the paint can. I drove to a nearby store to purchase another brush and returned to find Paul had almost painted one complete wall. The colour was definitely *not* 'butter yellow'. It was a bright lemon color that involuntarily puckered your mouth. I reassured Paul that it would look totally different when it was complete. I added white California shutters to get that fresh open feeling and a ceiling fan.

The first day after working a lengthy midnight shift, Paul crawled into bed exhausted. I kissed him good morning and goodnight and made my way downstairs to begin my day. An hour later I heard an anguished cry coming from upstairs and in a panic took two stairs at a time to the bedroom, expecting the worst. Paul lay on his back, his eyes the size of black-eyed Susans, the sun streaming in through the cracks of the shutters and illuminating the yellow room like a blazing fireball. "I'm going to get sunburned lying here," he groaned. "I can only do this if you string up a hammock."

It is impossible to eliminate the outdoor noises of dogs barking and children screaming or machinery such as lawnmowers and cars, but installing an air conditioner can be effective in both keeping the room cool in summer and blocking out unwanted noises. Supplying a ceiling fan is less expensive; it will also provide ventilation, and the hum of the fan will block out noise. Indoor noises, which are a part of daily living, such as kids playing; the washing machine, dryer or dishwasher; the phone ringing; or unexpected company are far more difficult for the officer to ignore and can cause him restless sleep and anxiety. The household duties can be put off until later but little ones cannot. The constantly reiterated "shh shh" is probably the first word your youngster will learn and take most seriously.

We had family and friends over to celebrate Sarah's third birthday. Each guest came through the door with brightly decorated parcels, bags and warm wishes. They were sternly greeted with "Shh shh" by little Sarah, who had developed a tendency to be bossy of late. They smiled at her peculiar greeting. A friend played the Lion King CD for Sarah, who became visibly upset, brushed past her father and angrily pushed the button to release the CD. "Shh, didn't you hear me, my Daddy's sleeping," she hissed angrily. Mark swung her up into his arms laughing, "Honey, I'm not sleeping today, I'm off work for your birthday." "Oh, good," she said, relieved. "I didn't know how I was going to keep all these people quiet."

Keeping young children quiet is probably one of the most challenging aspects of shift work. Plan some of your visits with family and friends for a midnight shift and you can return the visit when the officer is working afternoons or days. This is a good time to enjoy the programs and activities that your town provides, such as Moms and Tots, Toddler Fun, Tiny Tots, Gymnastics or Craft Fun.

I used to put the baby down after lunch and crawl in beside Tom. I'd get an hour's sleep. It was just nice being close to him, a feat that was extremely difficult with a growing family, and at times I had to use self-control to keep from talking or touching him. It's a great time to take advantage of a short nap to revitalize ourselves.

Another spouse commented:

The noise was difficult to handle when the kids were little but at least I felt I had some control. Now the front landing is filled with teenage shoes of every size and shape and the voices sound like front-end loading trucks and screeching brakes. We were fortunate enough to have Dad help finish the basement and soundproof it so that the massive bodies, voices and music could be somewhat contained. We set the ground rules when they were little and they are really good at sticking to them. RULE: Dad sleeping; be quiet or everyone goes home.

Planning and organization are essential to a police family. At the beginning of each new year when you are marking the officer's shifts and days off, take the time to draw up a separate calendar for family and friends. This way there will be no mistake about when the officer is home and sleeping or when he's at work.

"You have to be very disciplined," says Ken Venables, a staff sergeant for York Region Police. "Even though you hear the routine noises your family makes and you would love to get up and join them, you have to learn to block them out. Carla works shifts and the kids are older now, but it used to be really difficult. I would get up to join in the fun and activity and end up paying for it later."

Social Life

The most common complaint in the survey from officers' families is the impact that shift work has on their home lifestyle and their social relationships. Families become very proficient at calculating hours, with frequent familiar requests such as "wake me up about 5:00 and I'll join you for dinner" or "give me until 7:00 and I'll watch the kids play hockey." "Wake me up at 10:00, I have court" or "Don't make plans for Saturday, I took a paid duty." Rescheduling can often be an embarrassment but hopefully friends and family will be understanding even if the calendar they've been given is forever changing with added court, overtime and duties.

It was our niece's first birthday and my sister-in-law had spent weeks planning a garden party for her. She always called in advance to schedule and luckily it was the one time we could all attend together. The kids were off work and Paul had the weekend off; there would be no court on a Sunday and he promised he wouldn't take any paid duties. But as usual something came up. His transfer to traffic came through and he had to switch shifts two days before the party. Now he had to work afternoons and would miss it altogether. Even though I keep telling myself I'm used to it, I still feel disappointment and sometimes resentment. I learned that time management was essential in our marriage and we learned early to compromise.

Many officers feel socially isolated and out of touch with the rest of the world. Most events take place in the evenings and on weekends and it's difficult for the officer to participate. They miss out on social clubs, school meetings or just coaching their kids' sports teams. One spouse admitted that in the first few years of their marriage some friends became skeptical of the constant excuses and date changes and they just stopped calling.

Police spouses are forever counting the hours that the officer sleeps—always calculating whether they've had enough or too little and when to respect the officer's need for a "recovery time" after a long stretch of midnights or afternoons.

We pass each other in a dream state. She's just getting home from midnights and ready for sleep and I'm just getting up and not quite with it. Once she asked me to let her sleep until three and I thought she said to wake her up in three. I get so confused keeping track of the kids' schedules and hers that I'm always afraid I'll mix them up. Was that give Joshua two tablespoons of medicine at 3 o'clock or three tablespoons at 2 o'clock?

Order in the House

By placing a large blackboard or dry erase board by the telephone you can write down little reminders of activities and times. You can also leave each other those little "feel good" notes, like 'I love you', 'I miss you', 'Meet you on the back porch at 10'.

Officers' families have difficulty trying to keep a sense of order and tidiness in their homes. Housecleaning and chores can't always be done on the same day. Unlike other couples who develop a routine and choose to do their chores every Saturday, a police couple will learn to do them on a Saturday one week and maybe on a Wednesday the next. They learn to delegate and teach children at an early age to help with the overload, or things inevitably start to pile up.

I always had trouble keeping my kitchen tidy. It felt like I was chained to the stove. The kids and I would eat supper and just as the clean-ups were done, Don would wake up and I'd feed him and then clean up again. The kids learned to rinse their own plates and pile them in the dishwasher, then pitched in with the clean-ups. I started putting Don's meal on a dish to be microwaved and when he was finished he just had to rinse the dish and put it away. Each person cleaned up after themselves. Now that the teenagers have jobs and eat at different times, I'm glad I kept at them.

It might sound silly, but some of our worst fights were over an unmade bed. Paul loved to crawl into the bed after a midnight shift. For him, the more rumpled the covers, the more warm and inviting. I preferred a freshly made bed with the cool cotton sheets pulled tight and tucked in. When he awoke at 5:00 p.m. he left me a mangled mess of material—always a cause for the beginning of an argument that often parachuted into a full-blast marital dispute. When I look back, it was partially due to the 'neat' hangup I had, but mostly due to the feeling that my whole life was untidy. We worked out a plan. I resisted the temptation to make the bed in the morning and he pulled up the sheets and blanket in an attempt to make it look made. I finally invested in a down duvet that was easy to pull up and was both tidy and comfortable.

Police spouses are always looking for ways to minimize the effects of shift work. This allows for less stress and more time to spend together instead of on the house.

Holidays

Holidays are the most joyous times of the year for many families. Law enforcement families cannot always spend some of those most important days together, but they learn to appreciate the little time they have. Police families spend many a Christmas, birthday and anniversary without their loved one. Children learn at a young age that the officer's job is to protect the public daytime, nighttime *and* during holidays.

Officers envy the sweet slumber and joyous celebrations of society as they drive their cars through the city looking for suspicious activity. There is nowhere they would rather be than at home with their own families.

By applying great creativity along with patience and understanding, families can begin their own family traditions, creating grand memories for years to come. Sometimes just the anticipation of waiting for your spouse to arrive home and the preparation of a special meal can be as exciting as any traditional holdiay meal. It's all in what you make it.

Our most difficult Christmases were when the kids were between the ages of 3 and 10. Michelle and Trevor wanted to open their presents on Christmas morning with their father and that was far more important to them than the Christmas feast. It wasn't always easy— again we learned that patience is a virtue, and we worked around the shifts. Gifts weren't always opened first thing in the morning, but we kept busy by preparing a wonderful Christmas brunch. The kids printed little notes and attached them to tiny homemade gifts which they slipped into Paul's pocket before he went to work. You can imagine his pleasure in receiving these memorable surprises.

Police families feel blessed just to be together mentally and spiritually if they can't be together physically. Once again, they learn to use creativity to assist in providing a well-balanced home.

I knew were weren't going to have Christmas dinner together again this year, so rather than feel sorry for myself I decided to call a couple of other police wives to join me in a little project. We all chose one of our favourite recipes to cook and together, along with the children, we drove to the station with a full Christmas meal, candles, decorations and presents. Some of us still didn't get the chance to join our spouses in the feast but it was great watching the faces of those who could get in for a bite.

The Benefits of Shift Work

There are some very positive aspects of shift work that the whole family will benefit from. In a working society of flexible hours, parents who both work can enjoy sharing childcare responsibilities. Some police services allow officers up to seven days off at a time.

Caring for preschoolers makes for great bonding and is easier on the budget.

Elementary school children will enjoy the benefits of their shift-work parent when he joins them for school functions during times when most parents are working.

I have my own business. It was great that Steve had days off or could take time from his 'time-off bank' to go on school trips with Rachael. Once he took the bus with 20 mothers and he was the only dad who could be there. Rachael was so proud of her dad when he reached for the reddest apples that were up too high for everyone else to pick.

Officers' families can also enjoy the benefits of quiet day trips, or take holidays during weekdays when there is no traffic or confusion on the roads. By using their time off wisely and making an effort to find time to be with family and friends, the family will reap greater rewards.

Sometimes we used to pay a surprise visit to the kids at school when Paul was off shift. We would show up at lunchtime carrying a large wicker picnic basket filled with cheese, homemade salami, fresh Italian bread and berries in season. I would bring along glass wine goblets for juice, stoneware plates and stainless steel cutlery to be placed on the red and white checked tablecloth. We would drive to our town's small artificial lake and, along with the company of geese and ducks, we lay on that soft mossy grass and giggled and tickled the hour away.

As children become teenagers, making time to be together is much more difficult. They develop their own social lives, become more involved in activities and take on jobs. Michelle said, "I really miss Dad. I feel like I haven't seen him in weeks." This was from our 19-year-old, who, years earlier, used to ask if her Daddy was ever coming home. The greatest invention for a police family is the cell phone and Michelle takes full advantage of calling her father each night.

Try to make time to be together at least one night a week even if the officer is working on a straight seven-day shift. Make this a routine—it benefits everyone by allowing communication to remain open. Talking is not the only way to communicate. Sometimes just being together during a movie, working on a project or simply sitting down to share dessert is enough to let everyone know the 'lines are open'. Some of the greatest discussions take place during these times. Keeping a family together is difficult in a 'normal' type of lifestyle, so officers' families have to make that extra added effort. By not exercising this kind of routine, the family becomes detached and dysfunctional, which can lead to severe family problems.

Loneliness

In a police marriage the spouse often finds herself alone. Loneliness is probably the most debilitating problem of shift work for the officer's spouse. The officer's hours away from home for long stretches of time are even more difficult for spouses of undercover officers, who are away for weeks and months at a time.

I'm so sick of our marriage revolving around his job. What's the sense of being married if you're alone all the time. It's not enough time to nurture a relationship. I toss and turn when he's on nights and I know I'm going to wake up feeling tired and have difficulty functioning the next day. He comes home, sleeps all day, gets up for dinner and hardly says two words, or he's in a bad mood. He would rather just sit in front of the television and veg out. He says it's his way of relaxing before work but I feel as if I'm getting the remnants of the guy I married.

One police wife retold the story of a wife who had been married to an officer in the drug squad for eight years. They had just moved to a new neighborhood and the kids, aged 12 and 14, were having trouble adjusting. She had seen little of her husband, who was heavily involved in a drug heist. She worried constantly about him and the kids and then, with the move, she fell to pieces. She always felt physically exhausted, anxious, lonely and unloved. She didn't want to bother anyone with her feelings. She had forgotten how to look after the most important person of all, herself. Two months after the move she took her own life. Ironically, it was an overdose of drugs that killed her.

Self-discipline and self-confidence are redeeming traits for an officer's spouse. Time away from the officer allows her inner self to grow and develop; she becomes strong and self-sufficient instead of depending on family and friends for companionship. She learns to enjoy her own company by occupying her time with a variety of activities. When a spouse feels as if she is running the house alone and doesn't feel appreciated, she must remain positive. It's a tremendous time to pamper herself. Try a luxurious bath and a good book by the fire. Join a group once a week, go back to school, take crafts, painting, dancing, aerobics classes. The choices are unlimited. JUST DO IT. When you look in the mirror you must like who you see.

And as for Romance...

Finding time for intimacy becomes a principal marital adjustment for police couples, especially those with young children. Finding a few uninterrupted hours alone can be nearly impossible.

It just seemed she was either on shift, too tired after shift, the kids were still up or I was working. There was never any time to be close. It was hard enough sneaking in a few minutes to cuddle. It began affecting our marriage and we had to seek counseling. Finding time to make love is kind of like banking—you have to make time to pay your bills or you lose everything you've worked for.

Spontaneous lovemaking is not an impossibility; it just takes a more conscientious effort by both partners. Professionals agree that it's one of the most important elements holding any marriage together. Without intimacy, a police officer may find that the opportunities thrown in his direction are too tempting.

Be flexible. Scheduling times to be together may appear unromantic, but this method can also be a delicious way to anticipate the time you will finally meet.

I can't believe I ever did this. I called my husband at the station and asked if we could meet for lunch. I chose a small, steamy little restaurant in one of the city's back streets, where I told him I wasn't hungry for food and I slipped him keys to the hotel room next door. At first he looked confused, but then this great smile lit up his whole face. I told him to give me five minutes so that I could light candles and dress for the occasion. Don snuck up the back stairway and knocked with great urgency. I greeted him with a glass of chilled white grape juice and his favourite food delicacies. Don agrees, the element of surprise, naughtiness and spontaneity made it one of the most wonderful hours we've spent together.

There are some great books that assist couples in being creative in the bedroom. Popular books such as *101 Nights of Romantic Sex*, written by Laura Corn, with sealed pages of fun activities, can put a spark into any marriage. Or take along *The Great Sex Weekend* by P. Schwartz and J. Lever. A police couple must be experimental with intimacy, embracing different locations, enjoying each other any time of day or night, and in any kind of light.

We didn't have much money in our young parenting days and we celebrated special days with homemade gifts and cards. Our tenth wedding anniversary was fast approaching, and Paul and I talked about how wonderful it would be to go on a romantic weekend away, but once again it wasn't going to happen. Instead I decided to create a 'night away' at home. I traded with a friend to look after the kids for a few hours, and with a little ingenuity changed the whole look of the bedroom. I crafted 10 red hearts as my gift to Paul, each bearing a romantic desire or activity that Paul could redeem at any time. It was just as much fun planning as it was spending time together. We enjoyed the hearts so much I began making them for Valentine's Day, Christmas, Easter and birthdays.

Make time to take a weekend or a few days holiday away together. You'll find the separation from the kids will only make you appreciate each other more. Don't forget, when the kids are grown and gone and only the two of you remain, you don't want to wake up one day wondering who the stranger is beside you. Our goods friends Wendy and Al truly believe and practice a good marriage and family bonding.

Right from the beginning Al's always been first. We see our children as a gift given to us to nurture and educate and launch into life. We put each other's needs before our own and the kids find security in our unquestioning love for each other. What better way is there to teach kids than by example.

Days Off

Officers' spouses are not the only ones who may become lonely in a police marriage. In police departments where a police officer works seven 10-hour shifts, he can enjoy up to six days off at a time. If his spouse works and the kids are at school, this can be a lonely time for him too. By taking a different 'lifestyle' role and helping with household chores, an officer can help maintain that balance his wife has worked toward.

Unfortunately, socializing is usually limited to seeing the officers that he works with. This kind of relationship is healthy if carried on in moderation. Some officers find they need to fill their time with each other's constant company and end up with undesirable drinking buddies. Some choose to find companionship with the opposite sex, leading to intimacy and ultimately destroying the marriage.

I was just bored. Marie worked as a nurse for the hospital in town and I met her in the grocery store. We got talking and found we had a lot in common, what with weird shifts and all. She'd had a couple of bad relationships and wasn't really looking for anyone. We met for coffee just to fill in some time and became good friends and then it just kind of happened. It destroyed my marriage and I ended up with nothing. I'm more lonely now than I ever was. It was just one really big mistake.

An officer should enjoy his time off working on interesting hobbies, perhaps join a fitness club or volunteer his time to the millions of groups in his town that are begging for help.

When the kids were little I was invited to join the ladies on the street for tea. It was a great way for the kids and me to socialize. They loved my input because they were guaranteed to get a different perspective, and I learned everything from parenting skills to new recipes. I became more sympathetic to Melissa's role in the home.

Dump That Donut!

Shift work can be the cause of a number of health problems. The digestive tract is constantly being tried due to the unusual eating patterns, causing problems such as ulcers, bowel disorders and weight gain. The most serious problem is the increase in coronary artery disease. The old joke "Help! I need a cop—call Dunkin' Donuts!" (*EAP Digest*, Jan/Feb 1990) is not far from the truth.

We had a garage sale a number of years ago and sold an old pair of police boots to a neighbor. It's a standing joke that each time we meet Barry he shouts over the fence in puzzlement, "Great quality boots for workin', just can't understand why every time I put them on I end up at the donut shop."

Officers are known for their excess consumption of donuts and coffee. Due to the nature of their job, long hours in a police car attending unpredictable calls does not allow them the leisure of a quiet meal in their favorite restaurant. These officers resort to quick take-out meals that are high in fat, salt and calories—food that usually ends up cold or uneaten. They fill up on coffee and junk, assuming it'll get them through the end of a busy time. By not storing as many of the 'good' nutrients in their system they become tired and anxious and thus unproductive.

In the survey conducted, 70 percent of the spouses admitted that the officer was overweight due to a poor diet and that he found difficulty in developing good eating habits.

Dennis had a mild heart attack two years ago at the age of 46. He'd heard that an officer's mortality rate was higher than other occupations but he never paid any attention. He said he spent a lot of time sitting in a police car and found he was exhausted after seven days of a 10-hour shift. It took him a couple of days to catch up, so he would relax in front of the televison. He had difficulty shaking that 'not normal' feeling. He loved fried potatoes of any kind, especially the homemade fries from the chip truck near the station, and he drank at least 10 coffees a day. He never found the time to exercise. He was so lucky to get a warn-

ing. With a lot of reorganization and discipline we have all changed our lifestyle to help Dennis become a healthier person, but he's the one who's had to change most drastically.

Shift work is extremely stressful on an officer's system, and studies have proven there is a 60 to 70 percent increase in heart disease. Eating certain kinds of healthy foods at the right time can provide energy when needed and in turn provide proper rest. Building good eating habits, instead of eating "comfort" foods that temporarily allow the officer to feel more 'normal', will be helpful in avoiding many health problems.

In shift-work families, especially when both partners are working, shopping and organizing meals can become tedious and time-consuming. This is when your organizational skills are really put to the test. Luckily, we can enjoy the services of 24-hour supermarkets, and many restaurants are beginning to notice the needs of shift workers who eat their dinner in the morning and require midnight breakfasts.

There are numerous cookbooks that teach us how to prepare healthy and quick meals that are low in fat and high in fibre. Try easy and nutritional books like *Looneyspoons* by Janet and Greta Podleski and *The Lighthearted Cookbook* by Anne Lindsay. Television is inundated with nutritional cooking shows that demonstrate appealing and great-tasting meals.

Mealtime is an important time to be together as a family and to discuss the day's events. An officer's family must make an effort to spend this special time whenever they can—even during a snack time after the kids return from school or before bedtime.

Life on the Street: A Typical Midnight Shift

The majority of police spouses never experience the reality of being out on the road and dealing with people from all races, religions and social backgrounds. People who might be physically or psychologically ill, financially destitute, depressed, uncared-for, unprotected or alone. The true-life stories that police officers tell have usually been disguised, either with humor or by the omission of the cold hard details, to protect themselves and to protect their families. Any call can turn ugly in a fraction of a second, a routine night may become so busy there are not enough cars to take the load. Another night calls may be slow, one minute chaos and the next peace again.

To appreciate what a typical midnight shift in Toronto can be like and to see first-hand the types of situations that an officer must deal with, I decided to join in a ride-along. I had to talk myself into it because I wasn't sure I was prepared to see the bitter truth. I was protected and happy in what Paul calls "a little cocoon." My view of society was pretty decent and I closed my eyes to anything that wasn't.

I was fortunate enough to ride in three different divisions of Toronto, all of which are densely populated and high in crime. The most eventful evening was in 52 Division where Paul was stationed at the time. This modern brick building is situated in the Chinatown area, constructed of white brick with modern block glass windows and the illuminated police sign in both English and Chinese. This station houses approximately 392 employees, the majority of whom are uniformed officers. The geographical border runs as far south as Lake Ontario and as far north as Dupont Street. The area extends east as far as Jarvis and west to Spadina Road.

This large block of the city encompasses Chinatown, the Annex, the University of Toronto and Ryerson University, as well as the Yonge Street business section. Toronto is the largest metropolitan city in Canada. It contains multi-million-dollar businesses, a thriving arts and culture scene, very high income residential areas and low-income areas.

It is Saturday, September 26, an unusually mild evening. The officers are gearing themselves up for another busy night in the heart of the entertainment scene. The station is bustling, preparing for a change of shift, with officers coming and going, hurling insults that would turn your stomach in any other surrounding. They joke as they file out about 'keeping an eye on the hookers' and pulling a prank or two. Some discuss a meeting place for coffee. But coffee is not to be on the menu on this unpredictable night. The ride-along was arranged around Paul's shift. I would be out in a division car while he worked in the traffic unit from 11:00 p.m. to 7:00 a.m.

The officers beginning their shift generally change at the station. They go to the back counter for their gun, which is taken to a loading station and loaded in a steel funnel-like container mounted on a bulletproof stand. This protects the officers from any accidental discharge. They check their voice mail and replenish any supplies they might need for their briefcase, such as ticket books. Their reports are primarily conducted by phone or on the computer.

They meet on the second floor 10 minutes before starting time, in a large room with long wooden desks. This is the parade room. Times have changed; the word parade used to mean that the officers would form up in a single line, at attention, and would prove their equipment such as their memo books, night sticks and guns and would be inspected to ensure their uniforms were clean and they were fit for duty. This practice generally has not been used in the last five years, although some stations still maintain the custom. They are still checked for acceptable appearance. They must be clean-shaven, hair cut short, with a clean and crisp uniform and shiny boots.

Dan was the officer I was assigned to. In the next few hours he would witness a number of my vulnerabilities. I sheepishly admit that he saw just about every one of them, despite my promise to be tough.

I am asked to sign a Release, Waiver and Indemnity form before accompanying Dan on the road. It states:

I HEREBY ACKNOWLEDGE THAT I have been advised that there exists a risk of injury to my person and damages to goods in my possession as a result of my exercise of the permission granted to me in the above application.

I HEREBY FULLY ACCEPT AND ASSUME SUCH RISK. AND IN THE CONSIDERATION of the permission granted to me to accompany a member of the Toronto Police Service, I UNDERTAKE TO COMPLY with all regulations, directions and requirements of the Toronto Police Service and to obey the lawful orders and directions of any member of the said Service I may accompany.

Translated that simply means, "You could get hurt, hang onto your purse, and if any police personnel tells you to leave, run like hell." I begin a cowardly withdrawal but then I am distracted by Dan's proud tour through the station. I wish I'd worn running shoes instead of stylish black pumps.

In the main booking office the walls are covered with billboards spread with the smiling faces of missing children, disturbing photos of men and women who are being sought for heinous crimes, warrants for the arrest of people who could be your next-door neighbor. They give a full description, criminal act and location last seen or generally frequented. There is a chilly atmosphere in this room, what with the hostile eyes of photos, the rustling of papers from officers busy booking suspects, and the bellows and caterwauls from those already in the holding cells. All of this gives me a sense of curiosity and simultaneously the impression of snooping into someone's private affairs.

In 52 Division the men file into the parade room and casually take a seat. The sergeant and sometimes the staff sergeant enter the room and bring the evening's detail and update sheets. The sergeant will shout out a roll call for each officer to answer. As the officer answers to his name he is given his detail, which includes the number of the car he will be driving, the area he'll be working in, his partner and his designated hand radio. The badge number of each officer and the number of his handheld radio will be sent to the radio room so that the officer and radio can be connected in case of an emergency. When the radio mike is keyed in, the radio number pops up on the dispatcher's screen.

There is more than a healthy amount of bantering, poking, fighting and teasing that goes on during this time. It's a release, a comraderie toward a dedication they share to look out for and protect each other no matter what.

The sergeant briefs them on the events of the past day and on the night ahead. They are informed about any new drugs being used, new areas that must be observed, complaints, criminals to watch for, with full descriptions including info updates like missing children and any elderly missing from hospitals. They are updated on bank robber suspects and, occasionally, businesses where the burglar alarms are out of order. This is an imperative part of police work, enabling officers to continue good police work and ensuring their safety. The sergeant cautions them about their own safety, advising them not to become the next 'stat'. This briefing gives the officers an opportunity to address problems encountered on previous shifts and in particular areas.

It's the second last night before the end of the shift. The officers look weary; most have had little sleep, working through the night, some of them in court all day and working overtime, yet they must be equipped to handle any situation thrown at them for the next eight hours. At the end of the parade I am introduced by my first name. The officers politely smile in my direction. The sergeant adds that I am Stone's wife. I distinctly hear faint snickering and some throat-clearing. I am not sure if this is a good thing or not. The officers push back their chairs and, collecting their notebooks, troop past me to return to the front desk for the equipment they'll need that evening, including, radar, alkaline tester, shotgun and breathalyzer alert.

The last officer walks past with a wide smile. "You married that guy?" he chortled.

More easy laughter from the hallway and some under-the-breath comments I didn't quite catch.

I could have felt insulted but after living a police lifestyle I knew this was just their way to have a little fun; no harm meant. A coughing fit erupted from one police officer, who cursed midnight shift. He apologized: "I get a cold on day shift and just when it feels as if it's finally getting better and I've had a couple of days to recuperate I start midnights and it is impossible to shake." His partner threw his hands up in despair, "You watch, I'll get it afternoon shift and we'll pass it back and forth all winter, then I'll give it to my wife." Shift work and residing in close quarters with each other plays havoc with infections and airborne bugs.

2330 hours

Dan's office is a mere 3 1/2 feet wide by 5 feet long and 4 feet high, equipped with wheels. His rear seat acts as the outer office. I climb into the passenger seat. There are no springs left in the seat for support and I sink down so far I am almost doubled in half. At my left shoulder is a sawed-off shotgun, its ominous black body sticking straight up and its metal muzzle pointed toward the roof. Nestled against my left thigh is the emergency control center console, which separates the two of us in what feels like a cockpit. The console consists of a variety of buttons for emergency lights, sirens and radio controls. An MDT computer—the main investigative tool, consisting of a small monitor and downsized keyboard—is mounted in the center of the dash. The safety screen of Plexiglas and metal directly behind the seat is confining and claustrophobic. This space is more constricting than the cockpit of a small airplane. The back seat can only accommodate a medium-sized person, making it an uncomfortable place to sit. Even though the cars are cleaned regularly, a rank odor is always present, mainly from the number of unkempt urchins that regularly occupy the rear seat.

Dan tests the siren equipment, the emergency light buttons and the radio. The ritual of 'logging-on' with the radio dispatcher begins, with a distorted garble of words, as we slowly move into the heart of the city. It's a kind of cement zoo. Broad solemn buildings lunge upward like long black piano keys, their tinted mirrored windows lit by the street lights, creating a night-time dazzle. On hot summer days the officers only experience sunlight between 11:30 a.m. and 1:30 p.m. when the sun reaches its highest peak; the rest of the time they work in the looming shadows of these superstructures.

There is a garble from the radio. "Ar to corer Jon n Unisity hers at 1400ours…" translated to "At the corner of John and University, purse theft at 2345 hours…" We do not take the call. Another officer radios back that he is close to the area mentioned and will attend.

We move into the Duncan and Richmond Street area, the entertainment center of Toronto, and sit in bumper-to-bumper traffic. A profusion of car horns sound off like a delirious orchestra, rickshaws bawl out their wares to the pedestrians, there is a fist fight on the corner and I can hear hot dog vendors laughing. It is like watching a movie on a large screen.

Young shapely women in trendy, short, slitted black skirts or spandex pants and fit men wearing khakis and resplendent polyester shirts walk toward buildings that inhale and exhale an exploding cacophony of notes. One bar entices people by exhibiting a live fire-eating and flame-throwing one-man show on a small teetering balcony above the doorway, while another exhibits a go-go dancer on top of an entrance roof. The sirens, horns, music thumping, people shouting and brakes squealing make the city seem out of control and give me an alarming feeling of wanting to run while I still have the chance. The flurry of energy and excitement is impossible to digest.

2350 hours

We drive over to the red light district of the city. Dan pulls up alongside the sidewalk to speak to one of the hookers stationed on a small street just off one of the busiest intersections in the city. He opens my window and greets the young lady.

"Hi, doll," he says. "What are you doing tonight?"

A tall lean body thrusts her head of pumpkin orange curls and her massive alabaster breasts into my window.

"Why, you lookin' for a date?" she asks with a sarcastic grin.

"No, just working the night shift," he says and she nods in her customary way with the 'I know what you're doing and I know you know what I'm doing' game. Dan asks how her daughter has been and who's looking after her tonight. She extends her arms within inches of my face without ever acknowledging my presence and wags a long cranberry-colored nail at the officer. Ignoring his question she asks "Got a new one tonight, eh?" as she dislodges her anatomy from the window. With her goes the strong scent of cedar.

"Be good now," she taunts.

Once the niceties have been exchanged she politely takes a step back from the car, anxious for us to move along so business can resume. Dan explains that the women at times offer pieces of information to keep in their good books. He checks to see if there are any warrants for their arrest.

0030 hours

We have been slowly driving through the city streets watching the activity. My ears have become more accustomed to the commotion and I can better decipher the voice on the radio, although I can't do both at once. When the radio crackles I find I have to look at it to hear it. I am beginning to understand one of Paul's habits that makes me crazy. His ability to survey everyone that walks by, remembering what they were wearing and any peculiar physical features, and to hear what people are saying and still understand and contribute to our conversation. This is a skill that develops and is honed over years of watching the roads, looking for infractions, listening to the radio and their partner at the same time, and driving.

We pull up behind a car that has a sticker on its licence plate dated last year.

Dan pulls him over to a safe spot off the road, using the flashing police lights. As a safety precaution he gets out of the car and stands directly behind the driver's window to check the licence and ownership. He returns to the police car and runs the driver through the computer to check whether he has a record. He writes out a 105-dollar fine for failure to renew license. This is done while sitting in the police car, using the steering wheel as a desk and balancing the rest of the information either on his lap or on the dashboard. Thankfully this is a no-occurrence call. The driver is courteous but tries to talk his way out of a ticket. Dan says they are always nice until they realize they are getting one, and it can go downhill from there.

0040 hours

The radio is cleared for the next call. The dispatcher announces five men with bricks causing a disturbance.

"The suspects have left the scene," she reports in a strong, calm voice, "walking southbound on Yonge Street toward Queen." This is followed by a short description of the suspects. Another officer has received the call and is in the vicinity to respond.

0052 hours

Due to downsizing and cutbacks there is a shortage of officers on the street, but crime continues to climb. This shift reveals only five cars on the road for the entire night. Depending on the severity of an arrest, a party may be taken into the station for investigation, and that car goes out of service for about two hours. This increases the workload for the rest of the officers on the road. There are a number of calls that come over the radio tonight, from alarm calls to a young boy collapsing, but other officers, ambulance and firefighters are already in attendance.

0100 hours

A female calls 911 from her cell phone threatening to commit suicide. We are closest to the call. Dan sounds the siren and off we drive through the heavy traffic to the corner of two busy intersections where she claims to be. There is no one at the scene and I imagine the poor soul has already done herself in, bleeding to death and dragging herself to the nearest trash bin to die. I am beginning to feel panicky.

Dan is calm as he methodically checks dark corners, back alleys, up and down the sidewalks and doorways. There is no sign of her. I know she is out there somewhere; perhaps her cry for help is too weak for us to hear. Dan assures me it was probably a prank call, and his intuition is pretty strong. We call back the dispatcher to advise her there is no sign of the women in question and we leave the scene. He is right, of course, no one has reported a dead body, but I still wonder, "What if?"

0115 hours

You would think in a large city such as Toronto the chances of passing another police officer would be pretty remote. This night we coincidentally end up at the same corner as two other cars, one motorcycle, two officers on bicycles and two on foot. Happy to see each other, they converse in what seems like a coded language followed by laughter, more codes and lots more laughter. They discuss the big arrest of the previous evening, where two men climbed up pipes leading to an elite bar to steal expensive paintings and cash from the safe. It was a clean arrest but with lots of action. The officers speak lustily of the 'hot' bar scene and the ensuing fights. They anticipate a rowdy evening. Great I thought, a bunch of drunks in brawls and me in sensible pumps.

0130 hours

The dispatcher comes across the radio again. She needs a car to respond to a call. When it's a chaotic night the dispatcher's voice will sometimes call asking for anyone to respond to the call. A complaint has come in from a citizen that one hundred people are fighting in front of a frat house near the University of Toronto. One male has been pretty badly beaten up by members of a football team who were drunk and under age. We are in the vicinity. I reposition the pen that I have been holding in a weapon-like manner. I watch for signs of distress on Dan's face but see none.

"Happens each September," he says. "The first-year students get out of control with their new-found freedom." I nod in agreement. Little does he know Paul and I have just recently seen our daughter off to university for her first year. As we approach I observe a few guys standing over a body and a few more dragging a limp body from inside the house. I have an urge to run to the nearest phone to call home and make sure our teens are where they'd said they'd be. A couple of officers and a sergeant are already at the scene and have taken control before I get a chance to use my pen. A kind neighbor stops to thank us for responding to the call so quickly. The ambulance arrives to pick up the beaten and still body lying on the lawn. It is an unsettling experience, and I realize it is one of the reasons for Paul's grilling to the kids before they go out and his insistence on knowing a return time and a phone number.

0215 hours

We patrol the area to check on any disturbances or fights that might flare up but there are none. Students sit laughing and talking on front porches and curbs. We exit through the old subdivision and head back to the main street, where we encounter two male aboriginals eyeing a portion of the sidewalk, deliberating where to sleep for the night. September is warm enough to wear short sleeves and food is plentiful, but in just a few short weeks many of the homeless will find themselves fighting over heated grates and desperately searching for warm clothes and food.

Toronto has thousands of homeless people. We watch some of them wandering through the city, alone or in pairs, others bedding down on park benches or grass and some sitting in front of the bars and theaters begging for change.

0300 hours

The radio calls out a theft. The suspect has grabbed a lady's purse and raced off on a mountain bike. A description is given and an approximate whereabouts along with the victim's name and location. We drive around the area in hopes of catching the suspect, and although a number of bikers go by, none fit the description. The bike is probably long gone.

I am not the least bit tired—a little anxious perhaps but still expectant and excited.

I have felt the adrenaline rush a couple of times and it felt pretty good. We make a pit stop at the station, giving us time to stretch before returning to our little office. This time it feels more familiar, as I snuggle into my half of the cockpit.

0320 hours

Just as we pull out of the station driveway we hear the dispatcher's voice announce a stabbing. The call was sent by the victim from a telephone booth. Dan's body language changes. He turns on the siren, presses the small of his back into the seat and instructs me to hang on. We rush to the scene, through red lights and around corners, with great safety and control. Everything goes by in a whir. My heels dig into the car mats with so much force that my knees ache. I clench the armrest and hold my breath. I am near death, I just know it, I squeeze my eyes shut as we fly through intersections and barely skid over the potholes. Within three minutes we land the cruiser around to the front of the reported phone booth. Again there is no victim in sight. Dan gets out to confirm the phone number and check behind the booth and the building. No one in sight. We wait at the corner for a few minutes. A group of rowdy teenagers walk by without making eye contact.

There are a few smirks and whispers and it is obvious they've been drinking and are out looking to do a little mischief. Dan once again calls back to advise there is no sign of a stabbing in the area and that it was probably another prank call. We sit there for a few minutes but no one appears.

0350 hours

I am getting quite proficient at understanding the radio dispatcher's voice, so well in fact that I clearly hear the call for assistance coming from Paul, who has stopped some unruly speeders in the entertainment area. I freeze. I knew it! It was chancy riding on the same shift as Paul but I never believed anything would actually happen. I can't read his voice. It sounded calm but then perhaps it was to keep pedestrians from panicking, like a doctor who does not want to upset his patient when he's about to have a heart attack. I search for some sort of emotion on Dan's face but there is none.

"Is Paul okay?" I gulped.

"Yup," he responded. "We'll just pop over to see what's up." Pop over is not exactly the term I'd use. We arrive in about a minute and a half. Great, I thought, this is the part where the doctor doesn't want to tell you that you're dying. We find Paul standing in the center of a ring of young men having a dispute. Dan bolts from the car, leaving me paralyzed in the seat. Within seconds the street is lit with flashing red lights, as officers from both 52 and 51 Division respond to his request for backup. Their entrance alone is enough to dispel the group of rowdies looking to fight with an officer.

This incident is a little too connected to the heart. This job holds too many close calls and possibilities. One minute we're sharing a few anecdotes and the next we're screaming through the city, not knowing what awaits us. There is nothing in between. I guess I've had enough. The incident with Paul has stressed me more than I expected, and I really just want to say goodbye to police work and get back to my safe cocoon.

0430 hours

Calls have come across the radio in the preceding hour—a 14-year-old unconscious, an attempted suicide, a domestic, four traffic accidents, a possible drug deal at an apartment park area and another fight. Is there anyone living a normal existence in this city, sitting in front of the television in their pajamas, eating popcorn with their doors locked and the lights dimmed? With ride-alongs the officer is able to pick and choose the calls to attend. If a call required Dan's assistance and I could be put in jeopardy, he could drop me at the side of the road and continue on. Luckily, it was a busy night without any life-threatening calls.

I have loved the endless fizz of the city with its theaters, its lake front, the tourists and even its oddities. I have spent weekends in hotels where I never wanted to sleep in case I'd miss the ceaseless action of the night life. I have been a working city girl and traveled the pavement to and from the stupendous office buildings, and I have pressed my nose against shop windows countless times. My romantic view of the city will never alter, but now there seems a quiet sinister shadow just below the surface. I feel more like a visitor than a resident.

0500 hours

Thankfully, Dan is called to the station to pick up a prisoner and transport him to another station. Paul can leave early to take his physically and mentally fatigued wife home.

Dan and I say our goodbyes. I find I have developed a bond with this young spirited police officer, who has a wife and little children waiting at home. He treats his job with great enthusiasm, diplomacy and respect. His young eyes have seen more than they should.

I drag myself in the back door and through the station to the front where I will meet Paul. I wear a brave front of achievement, my pen still clasped in one hand and my notebook in the other. I am tired, my feet hurt and my brain aches. I am suddenly jolted into alertness by a moaning body draped over the counter. He too has dragged himself into the station, but only after being repeatedly stabbed. His blood drips down the wooden counter and onto the floor. The sirens from the ambulance outside the door subside. I turn away, praying for the normalcy I once knew.

0520 hours

The drive home, which is usually 45 minutes, seems like an eternity. I try to reveal the events of the evening to Paul but I am exhausted. Everything is jumbled and confusing.

Sunday, 1000 hours

I sleep through my standard 7:00 a.m rising. I know with my first stretch that it will be a long day. The sun pushes its way through the slats of the shutters and reflects on the yellow walls like a sunburst. The night's events slowly and menacingly come back to me and I can't get back to sleep. Leaving Paul peacefully snoring, I plod down the stairs to the kitchen. My head seems fat, as if I am suffering from an evil hangover, and my lids sit woodenly over my eyes. I am grateful my children are teenagers and sleep in late, grateful I am not in a profession where I have to work shifts, and especially grateful that I am not a police officer.

Tonight when Paul readies himself for the last night of midnights I watch with a different kind of respect. I kiss him a few seconds longer and he smiles in appreciation. I am secretly thankful to say goodbye, and after securing the door I dash up the stairs to crawl under the still-warm quilt.

An Evening in 51 Division

I had previously been to 51 and 41 Divisions for short night shifts. The evening in 51 was one I'll never forget. The officers work in a depressing pale yellow brick building which, at 53 years, is one of the oldest in Toronto. It's nestled in an Ontario Housing complex and sits like a target in the middle of Regent Park. The occasional gunshot can be heard from inside the station. In this division are the majority of the city's homeless.

One officer describes 51 Division as "a place where officers should only stay five years or less or they risk getting into a rut from having to deal with so many negative people and situations. This can result in the officer acquiring a negative attitude as well."

The cold weather didn't seem to affect the residents of the division, other than forcing those who had a home to stay inside and those who did not, to find shelter in hostels or on city grates that could provide a little warmth. The majority of residents in this division are destitute—crack heads, cheap prostitutes, alcoholics and many homeless. Rarely do the officers frequent the more elite residential area in the north end. Working in 51 is depressing. It lacks the glitter of the entertainment section of the city, the tall elegant buildings and young lively people. The buildings here are old and neglected and the residents are disorderly. One police officer commented that these victims of poverty and despair would pass their maladies of colds, flus and diseases onto the police officers who dealt with them continuously, and they in turn passed them back and forth to each other. There is more of a risk of being pierced with dirty needles or infected by tainted blood in this division.

The streets were quiet and within a couple of hours a severe snowstorm began to deluge the city. We had only had one call, a bedraggled woman casually walking back and forth at the edge of the road. Sergeant John Martin stopped to see if she needed assistance. She would not admit that she was soliciting, but upon being questioned she produced a form that stated she was not allowed to do so in the vicinity. Sergeant John Martin asked her to leave and without any altercation she was on her way. We circled the same city block for quite some time before I realized we were passing the same spot where he had previously spoken to the young lady.

"She'll be back," he assured me. He must be wrong, I thought; she was co-operative and even likable. But within half an hour we drove by the same spot and there she was. I was unprepared for the sudden stop. He jumped from his car and grabbed her arm, ordering her to lean up against the police car, where he quickly handcuffed her and then guided her into the back seat. He spoke kindly, informing her she was under arrest, and read her her rights. Facing the reality of spending time in jail she suddenly turned ugly, kicking the back seat and screaming obscenities at both of us. I was too nervous and too embarrassed to look behind me and focused on the dispatcher's voice.

At the station she was searched by a gloved female officer and placed in a holding cell until the paperwork was completed. Paperwork for booking can take anywhere from 2 to 12 hours. The cells were filled, and officers worked diligently to finish up the most tedious part of their job.

I overheard one officer in an intense conversation with his wife.

"What are you mad for? I can't help it, I got a call at the end. You know I just can't leave it," he said dejectedly, shuffling through the stack of papers in front of him.

"Just tell them I'm sorry and we'll try to get together again next week when I'm off."

There was silence and he hung up the phone. I guess she'd hung up on him. I certainly felt her frustration, but when I looked at his downcast face as he began the long hours of grueling work ahead of him, now with an angry wife waiting at home, it certainly gave me a different perspective.

The arrested female could be heard cursing throughout the station.

"She's a live one, this one," the booking sergeant smiled as he directed her to a more permanent cell. I was still feeling a little sorry for her. She seemed all right; that is, until she spat in the booker's face. He coolly wiped it off with a paper towel and continued to record the contents of her pockets. A five-dollar bill, a court form and a crack pipe. She stomped up and down, then ran to the bathroom to be sick. The booker invited her to sit back down and she gave him a conniving smile.

"No problem," she laughed, her ample rear finding a spot on the wooden bench.

"You guys got nothin better to do, eh? Why aren't you out there bustin' the guys that are really breakin' the law?" She kicked an imaginary object on the floor.

"Guess what?" she added. "I've got a secret."

"What's that?" he replied.

"I've got Aids."

The booker looked down at the paper towel he'd just tossed into the garbage can.

How could I have been such a poor judge of character? I once prided myself in the ability to see beyond looks and straight into the heart within the first few minutes of meeting someone.

Paul had told me stories of being spat on, punched, scratched and kicked, and until now I had thought them unpleasant but never threatening. If I'd held a night stick that night I'm sure she would have felt its sting. I couldn't understand how the officers could show such restraint. After she was led to her cell I asked the officer how he could take that kind of abuse.

"Guess you just get used to it," he replied. "We have to protect them from the rest of society, themselves and our own backsides."

I concluded that I felt less threatened in a room of blue than with the citizens on the street. There was no doubt in my mind that I would never have made a good police officer. I felt a greater appreciation for the job Paul does. I wouldn't go as far as polishing his boots, but I now send him off with a loving kiss and try to maintain a positive attitude even when he works late. As one officer's spouse adamantly remarked after her one and only ride-along, "I'll never do it again. I knew before I even got in that car it would be a night I'd never forget. How can anyone in their right mind really enjoy this kind of torment and mistreatment?"

Demands of the Job

Law enforcement is not like other jobs. We have seen the effects of one of the demands—shift work—but there are many other complexities that make it unique. The emotional and political struggles that officers encounter daily both on the street and within the department will ultimately affect their home life.

Paul had been on the job for a number of years and though I still worried about him on occasion, I became somewhat accustomed to our chaotic way of life—that is, until one day near the end of spring. Paul arrived home to announce he had accepted an assignment working in the red-light district, which had pronounced homosexual activity and Aids. He was shocked at the burst of anger that bolted from me, as I blasted him with, "NO WAY, YOU'RE NOT DOING IT! OVER MY DEAD BODY!" He argued that this would help broaden his knowledge of police work, but all I could see were the horribly vivid pictures that ran through my mind. He started the following day.

Promotion

Each assignment in police work carries its own distinctive stresses. Not all officers are looking to try various posts, but for betterment and promotion, it is to their advantage.

My husband volunteered to be part of the Public Order Unit. He

was called in whenever they needed him, whether he was work-
ing or at home. He hoped this would lead to a promotion but it
became just another attachment to the job and another thing
that made our home life more difficult.

The undercover unit is an aspect of police work that can be exciting and colorful. It feels totally different from uniform work to the
officer and it's just the kind of duty that will send the spouse right
around the bend. Although there are varied shift changes, the majority of the work is done at night; that along with the increased amount
of risk puts more stress on the family.

When William was working undercover he was gone for four
straight weeks. Someone from the department would call once a
week to let me know he was fine, but no one ever asked how I
was doing. I was not fine. We had one daughter and twin boys,
and one twin had a serious medical problem and we had to
spend a lot of time at the hospital. I depended a lot on my moth-
er and my sister. I felt like my world was falling apart. When we
would finally see William it was never for very long. I felt con-
fused, I missed him, I was mad at him, I loved him, I hated him
for being away all the time. He was missing out on the kids and
I felt so alone.

In most jobs, promotion is regarded as a reward for good performance, but with police work, even if the officer follows the appro-
priate avenues, he can become quickly disillusioned due to the
changes in policies, financial restrictions and interdepartmental politics that can put promotional opportunities on hold. They find they
become 'stuck' at the same level for longer than they anticipated and
become discouraged. Job evaluation is determined by the officer's
experience, additional education, how well he functions under stress-

ful situations and how he gets along with his workmates. Once promotional exams have been written, the officer is officially promoted and put on a waiting list where he waits his turn. Sometimes this can take months.

Now everyone has the chance to write the promotional exams, but Paul remembers a time when you used to have to work through the ranks of uniform, old clothes (undercover) and in the detective office to be qualified or 'rounded' enough for promotion. If you didn't know someone in the higher ranks it was hard to move around the squads but once you were in, you could go from section to section and then back again. Some officers may stay out of uniform and in special squads for years, keeping the new officers from acquiring any experience.

It was really hard on all of us when he wanted to make sergeant. That was over 15 years ago but he clearly remembers the heartache he went through. He knew that what was right wasn't always right for the department, but he lost it when they passed him over for a promotion and gave it to another guy who didn't deserve it but was a good drinking buddy with the staff sergeant. It took a long time for him to get over that one. He felt cheated and thought he looked like a failure to his family and the guys at work.

Police work has become more specialized, offering areas of advancement from administration to criminology, corrections to public safety, and these areas usually require additional training. Officers seek to enrich their skills by enrolling in courses to help them ascend more rapidly. Although promotions may be a long way off, officers 'buckle down' to the added demands of homework and exams and once again distance themselves from their families.

Sean took courses at a local college for three years. He worked it around his shifts so that after day shift he could go directly to his class, he'd book time off before afternoon shift and on mid-nights he'd get up, have a quick dinner with us and then drive off to class. I got so fed up with work, school, court, work, school, court and no time for the kids and me. Sean was stressed to the limit and I even tried helping him with homework so I could spend some time with him, but eventually I became resentful. When he finally finished all his courses he expected it would give him a foot in the door immediately but he was disappointed to learn he had a long wait. I was glad because we had a lot of repair work to be done to our relationship.

It used to be that the first thing reviewed by the Promotion Board was the officer's sick bank. If an officer had had more than several days off a year, he wouldn't be considered for promotion, but now work-related courses and special training help the officer better prepare for the variety of fields available. When the time comes, it always helps to provide the department with proof that he has tried to better himself.

Many officers who begin police work as patrol officers are content to continue in this career indefinitely. They love to be out on the street, in the middle of the action, where dealing personally with the public gives them their greatest satisfaction. They abhor being caged in an office with the paperwork and the politics. Some officers who have joined the department with university degrees are quite content to remain on the street. Once an officer decides what aspect of police work he enjoys most, he can work toward being the best he can be. As the spouse of an officer, some of your satisfaction should also come from being the very best that you can be, including supporting any career moves your police spouse feels are necessary.

Climbing the ranks in the police department may not always result in the glorified positions that some might think. A sergeant's career comes with a multitude of its own stresses, from the organizing of shifts to keeping officers content by pairing them with partners they get along with. As in a marriage, officers can have personality conflicts, clashes and disputes, and may prefer to work with certain people who don't 'ruffle their feathers'. Sergeants also rotate—one remains in the office to do administrative work while the other supervises the officers on the road. There is an immense amount of added responsibility that comes with this job, which is not reflected in the paycheck, and sergeants are rarely appreciated for their administrative talents. Once promoted, the person usually changes substantially, due to the increase of responsibilities, as well as beginning to feel like a middleman, who receives pressures from both those he manages and those he must report to.

One sergeant's wife related the disappointment she felt at the Christmas party after her husband's promotion.

Being at the top comes with a price that can be very lonely. It used to be so much fun socializing with everyone in Ryan's old platoon. A lot of us had been together for years and knew each other really well. Everything changed when Ryan got promoted. We sat with the other sergeants and their spouses and I got the feeling that even though they were polite, they were uncomfortable around us. What really hurt my feelings was a comment made by one friend, "Nice dress the sergeant's wife is wearing," as I was leaving their table.

Endless Work

All officers are inundated with excessive paperwork, long working hours, with court time and overtime, which causes a great deal of strain on the family and competes with the marriage for attention. They rarely put in a mere 40-hour week. If a person is arrested and brought to the station for investigation, the arresting officer stays until the work is done. He cannot leave in the middle of an arrest or a call because his shift is over.

It took a lot of getting used to. The job was forever interfering with our plans. I had always thought that if he had to choose between us or the job, he'd pick the job. I finally came to the realization that he couldn't do much about it and neither could I. He had made two very large commitments. Some people can't even manage one. It's not the kind of job that you can put aside for a day or two. It is consuming but very rewarding for him. I had to learn to step back, become more independent, and let him do his work without me always nagging him.

Criticism and Complaints

Because of the officer's continuous exposure in the public eye, he is set up as an immediate target, subject to criticism. Citizens look to the officer's strength when they need help, but when he must make an arrest or give out a ticket, they are no longer supportive. They feel their rights are being taken from them and they become disagreeable. An officer must maintain control and continue to keep the peace; unfortunately, though, no matter how well he handles a call there are still people who complain. Complaints can take the form of verbal abuse channeled directly at the officer, or a citizen might take it one step further and issue a complaint to the police department.

The officer feels he has to deal with a 'damned if you do, damned if you don't' outlook. The department's administration requires rigid discipline and often offers inadequate support.

Paul can put in a busy day at his traffic unit and never encounter a disgruntled citizen, but on another day he might only give out one ticket and it will be to an enraged citizen who demands his badge number and races to the station to file a complaint.

All complaints are taken seriously and are reviewed by the Public Complaints Investigation Bureau. Each complaint is diligently followed up and responded to, and can become an officer's nightmare. The complaints can range from misinterpretation of an officer's remarks to physical threats. Quite often, a citizen will complain against the officer who charged him in the hope that this may even the score or cause the charges to be dropped.

> *Bob knew when the sergeant called him into his officer that an angry female from a previous call had filed a complaint against him. He had needed to physically restrain her from piercing her sister with the end of a sharp spade. What she neglected to tell the sergeant was that Bob had succeeded not only in restraining her but also in calming the rest of the family. She put him through hell. She cried assault and was determined to get back at him, but thankfully her record showed she'd been in trouble before. This was her way of retaliating.*

Receiving a complaint is never positive, but too many can cause an officer to be sent to a another division and may close some doors to advancement. He may be looked upon with disfavor. It is inevitable that if an officer is out there, working hard, he will step on some toes. What he needs is a sounding board when he arrives home, someone he can lean on when it seems that everyone is 'out to get him'.

Always on Call

Officers who work in smaller towns and remote areas have the added responsibility of being on call 24 hours a day. Their home life can be disrupted at any time of day or night and for a myriad of reasons. Their name, their family, their phone number and the location of their home becomes common knowledge to residents. These families sit at the edge of their seat every time the telephone rings or a beeper goes off. They have been threatened and some have been singled out for being a law enforcement family.

We had a barbecue last summer celebrating our daughter's engagement. We invited a few friends and neighbors and some family flew out for the occasion. Just as Mat was flipping the steaks, the cell phone rang. I leaned over and pleaded for him not to answer, but I knew he had no choice. He received a call for a violent domestic and I knew he'd be gone for hours. He handed me the utensil and left me to finish barbecuing, entertaining and explaining. I could never rely on him to be around, and even though I've tried to prepare myself for the unexpected I still get disappointed. I tried to look at the positive side—at least everyone got a chance to see him, we were celebrating a wonderful occasion and we all had a great time.

With Paul in the traffic unit of his division, our family now faces a different kind of stress due to the added amount of time he's away from home. Giving out tickets eventually brings about more court appearances and more paperwork. This additional load, along with the long drive to and from the city, makes Paul tired and grumpy and unavailable for chores or quality time with his family. Any conversations are on the run or consist of some incomprehensible murmurings after the lights are out. Now that the kids are older, with jobs, school and their own social lives, they admit that they don't get much chance to visit with Dad. We decided that we would *make time* to be around when he was home. It meant more rescheduling and rearranging, but the extra effort has made all the difference toward a closer bond and a happier relationship as a family.

Justice or Injustice?

Officers have their share of frustrations, and one of the most difficult is with the criminal justice system where they are confronted with outcomes of cases that seem unfair and unjust.

After a day or two in court dealing with what the officer thought was a solid case and one that he may have labored over for many weeks, he may find the case is thrown out because of a technicality.

When Derek, Paul's younger brother, worked as a parole officer at Collins Bay Institute, the two would have some pretty enraged discussions, loaded with strong arguments on both sides. One brother worked to 'catch and put the bad guys in jail' and the other worked at 'getting them out', but they both agreed that the judicial system had to change, and provide tougher laws and harder sentences for criminals.

Paul had a case where a female had been badly beaten twice by her boyfriend and out of fear didn't want to press charges. The boyfriend continued his abuse; he finally succeeded in stabbing her in the throat repeatedly and leaving her to die in the hall outside her apartment. It took some persuasion, along with protection, to convince her to press charges against him. When the court date finally arrived the concrete case (i.e., one with solid evidence) was dismissed because of some ridiculous glitch.

That kind of disillusionment discourages and angers an officer, sending him home to his family in a furious state, barking about the injustice of it all. This becomes a disconcerting experience for both the officer and the family, who look to the justice system as a symbol of protection and to laws that are right and true, and worthy to be upheld.

On the lighter side, our family has a much better understanding of the laws and the system, so that following the news or reading the paper has become far more interesting.

Saints Required

The restraint that an officer uses in the course of his working day can be akin to that of a saint. He is faced with situations where he becomes an expert at reducing friction and defusing tension before the condition worsens, and that takes a lot of self-control. Some calls are hard to handle without becoming emotionally involved, depending on the situation and how close to his own life it may be at the time.

My wife attended a call where a father and son had been arguing over an accident the young boy had gotten into with his father's car. The boy was testing his father to the limit and the father, having had a few drinks, was ready for a good fight. The son raised his fist and it was all the father needed to punch him right in the mouth. The son took advantage of his father's unstable condition and, with all of his 18-year-old strength, pushed his dad into a brick wall, knocking him unconscious and unknowingly causing him head injuries. When my wife attended the call she was reminded of an ugly fight that had ensued between me and our son Geoff just a few days before. Geoff was upset that I wouldn't give him any money, but I didn't feel he'd earned it, therefore, he didn't deserve it. After some pretty foul language from him, he had walked up and chested me, looking for a fight. I walked the other way and endured the snide remark under his breath about 'being a chicken'. What could have developed into a similar situation was what really upset my wife and brings her to tears any time Geoff and I argue.

An officer that shows that kind of restraint at work can turn it into a positive quality at home. By using his intuition and common sense, he can defuse arguments between kids and parents in his own relationships. He can intervene before the fuse gets too short and with his ability to respond quickly, beginning with the emotion, the thought and then the action, he can channel any aggression in a more positive direction. Officers have a natural skill that many of us have never learned to adapt.

Always a Cop

Unlike some occupations, an officer has difficulty leaving his responsibilities at work. The expression 'once a cop, always a cop' is based on truth. The unwritten code of behavior that officers live by becomes a part of them as surely as the personality they begin developing from infancy. When a situation presents itself, whether on the job or off, a part of the officer's brain automatically responds. Families may never have the opportunity to be on patrol with an officer, but they walk that shaded area between off-patrol and on-duty daily with their own spouse or parent. Many have witnessed him in action on numerous occasions, but still can't become accustomed to the police mentality.

We were driving home from a family reunion. It was about two in the morning and we were both really tired when this jerk behind us blinded us with his high beams, then sped up and made an unsafe pass, pulling sharply in front and slamming on his brakes. He'd speed up then slow down, weaving in and out of his lane. I closed my eyes and prayed we'd get home safely. I knew Dave wasn't about to let this one go. He placed a call to the nearest police station, advising them of a drunk driver. Dave followed the driver until the police responded. We drove 20 miles out of our way and I was a nervous wreck. I was mad that he couldn't just let the police take over. He explained that he wasn't about to let a drunk driver get away with murder. I knew he was right, but I still had a bad taste in my mouth from last time, when

Dave accosted a young man 'skulking' around one of the neigh-bor's houses late one night and it turned out to be the neighbor's brother who'd lost his key and was looking for a way in.

Some stories sent in by police families were amusing, and others were thrilling accounts of their experiences. One spouse recalls her husband's suspicion upon hearing noises coming from their kitchen. He snuck down the stairs only to find their son, the 'midnight snack-er', helping himself to the leftover turkey and completely taken by surprise when his dad, in 'Fruit of the Loom' briefs, came around the corner with a toilet plunger in his hand.

Another spouse recalls hearing the glass doors to their family room slide open late one night. She tried to wake her police husband out of a deep sleep to warn him that someone was breaking into the house, but he assured her that he heard nothing, that it was probably just the wind. The next day they found their stereo and television set had been snatched by the thieves.

An officer will handle a situation in the same manner as if he were working even if he is with his family. He has a responsibility to uphold the law 24 hours a day. Families who have never seen their spouse or parent perform his duties at work have most surely seen him perform in some way when they're together.

The night before our wedding we were at a bar and my fiancé noticed a man pointing a gun through the bar window from out-side. Roger felt it was his duty to go out and do something. I was never so scared in my life. I figured he'd be killed for sure and there would be no wedding. Believe me, I got cold feet that night.

Our experiences as a police family have been numerous and excit-ing. Paul is not an 'over-zealous' cop, but he does believe that if someone is breaking the law, it doesn't matter when or where, it is his duty as a police officer and a citizen to do something about it. Our children have been privy to several incidents where Dad has had to keep a situation under control until another officer arrived. They've seen him direct traffic at an accident, apprehend a thief in a major department store, stop a knife fight and drive a drunk home. The kids have some pretty exciting stories to tell their friends, and some sad ones too.

We were traveling north on the highway on a long weekend when we noticed cars pulling over to avoid a body lying on the road. A teenager had been hit by a car. The emergency response had not yet arrived, so Paul pulled safely over to the side of the road, grabbed our hockey blanket and ran to the pedestrian. He requested the assistance of another driver to block the lane. Paul covered the boy, cautious not to move him; he checked for a pulse and performed CPR. With our noses pressed to the car window, we each said our own silent prayer. The teen died in Paul's arms even before the emergency unit arrived. We were all devastated.

Once, when the kids and I visited the Canadian National Exhibition where Paul worked, a large crowd surrounded two teens fighting with knives. Paul calmly worked his way into the circle and disarmed them both. Our two little children and I were all sure Dad would never make it out. Even though the kids were quite young at the time they have never forgotten that incident, and though they jokingly refer to Dad as the "hero in the house," they most lovingly and respectfully mean it.

Being present when Dad 'jumps into action' can be a scary experience, but it allows us to appreciate the kinds of calls he deals with at work and it enables the kids to understand some of the reasons for Dad's grumpiness and distancing. It also strengthens family bonds by providing a shared experience, and shows us the pride he takes in his work.

My husband was helping out at our daughter's hockey game. The coach had to stop the game a few times to request a couple of quarrelsome spectators be removed because they were swearing, throwing wrappers and bottle caps, and spitting at the players on the bench. When they refused, Jim identified himself as a police officer and asked them to leave or he would charge them with causing a public disturbance. The coach was happy to get back to the game and the kids thought it was great. And our kids thought their dad was a star.

A number of years ago our family traveled to a large city for our holidays. Paul drove into a gas station to fill up when a young punk sped up in front of him and cut him off to reach the pumps first. Paul stuck his head out the window and asked why he did that; the teen laughed and spat out some foul language, just loud enough for the kids to hear. Recognizing that the teen was looking for a fight, Paul drew back into the car, fuming as he waited for him to finish. When the teen came out of the station he casually walked around the back of our car and tossed a bottle of oil into the driver's window, dousing me, the kids, the car and blinding Paul. But Paul didn't need to see when he jumped out from the car, grabbed the insolent teen and wrestled him to the ground. We could hear groaning but couldn't see who was doing it. The kids thought it was Dad and started to cry and I ran into the gas station to call police. We got a good sense of what an adrenalin rush felt like, except a lot of it was fear.

Police officers do not take any unnecessary chances that might cause their family harm. They know when to take action and when to back off if it looks dangerous.

It has only happened a couple of times where my wife was with me when I felt it was really necessary to take charge. I worry more that something might happen to her. It's better to drop her off at a safe place like a restaurant or something and get her to call police while I stay with the suspect. My wife doesn't like me to get involved because she's worried I'll get hurt.

It is especially difficult for an officer to master relaxation methods because of his immediate and instinctive nature, but the ability to shift from the work to the home mode is crucial. Those who can't fight off the urge to be 'on duty' all of the time are candidates for an eventual burnout.

Police officers and their families who learn to adjust and accept the way police work dominates their lives can continue to develop strong and healthy relationships.

Free from Fear

On June 22, 1994 in Willowdale, Ontario, ten thousand officers from across North America, South America and Europe stood in the 90-degree heat to offer their fraternal support, in their close-knit tradition, to a fellow officer. The rigid formation of dark blue stood row on row in deafening silence.

We watched as a pale Constable Mike Leone, eyes cast downward, marched past us carrying the square blue-velvet pillow that cradled the hat once belonging to his partner. The sun reflected off badge number 114, which had been assigned to Todd Baylis, who was shot in the head as they chased a man through an apartment building into a dark courtyard outside. Officers faltered, some fainting from the unbearable heat or from the exhaustion of having worked a night shift, followed by morning court, and others reeling with the sickening grief and realization that it could have been any one of them.

I wondered if they heard my sobs over the measured police boots falling on the asphalt or if they heard my desperate prayer, "Please, please don't let this happen to us!" It was weeks before I could shake the tragedy, it festered in every move I made and small chore I performed. Once again I became a victim of fear. I panicked each time Paul dressed for work, clinging to him in desperation. The mourning process was drawn-out and painful, just as though I had lost a member of my own family. I had to force myself to continue my life with some sense of normality. I kept asking myself, "Why did I marry a cop?"

I wondered if the same question entered Kim Hancox's mind on the night of Wednesday, August 4, 1998, when she was informed that her husband Bill had been brutally murdered by a knife in a surprise ambush.

The news was immediately broadcast across all police radios, informing officers of the tragedy. Paul and I were on the cell phone with each other when the broken voice of the dispatcher came across, and in horror we clutched the receivers to our burning ears in an attempt to fight back the sickening grief that enveloped us.

We attended the funeral in support of Bill's family and friends, and all police officers and their families around the world. I stood on the roof of a nearby school to witness the pitiful scene and to once again relive every police spouse's worst nightmare.

A cloud of uniformed officers stood at ease, white-gloved hands like wings of doves perched over their belts and chins thrust forward in an attempt to show what little strength they had left after three hours in the heat and humidity. The blood-red uniforms of the Royal Canadian Mounted Police stood out as a sharp reminder of the tragedy.

Overcome with deep sorrow, Kim Hancox stood at the church door, her left hand clenched into a fist over her swollen stomach, pregnant with their second child and without the comfort of her tiny two-year-old whom she had left at home. Kim watched as her husband's partner, Detective Constable Vince Henderson, holding back tears, walked by her, head down, cupping his slain friend's cap, with badge number 6780, on the blue cushion.

The scene from where I stood could never be described in words; it was suffused with emotion, which pushed its way up through one's veins, pounding just under the surface of the skin, anxious to erupt. The emotion arose from the grim and weeping faces in the crowd, the vibrations of the drum beat, the solemn march of the officers and the painful absence of Bill Hancox. I heard the silent screams from the crowd, "It could have been my friend, my lover, my husband, my son!"

Kim Hancox's aching words about her husband are engraved on our hearts. "My only hope is that the tragic death of my best friend will not be in vain and that his memory will not soon fade. Bill deserves justice in his life. He worked hard to protect our safety and he needs our help to ensure justice prevails."

How to Survive

Despite such tragedies, when officers are asked, "Aren't you afraid you might be killed?" they usually respond with a casual "it could happen to anyone" or "I don't really think about it."

We wonder if officers don't have to be a little bit crazy to set themselves up as heroes, but they all seem to have an unbelievably great desire to do their small part in enforcing the law. If this is the occupation they choose, then we have a responsibility to support them.

Officers are taught not to think about death but to fight to survive. Unfortunately, no one teaches the spouse how to survive. The nature of this high-risk profession and its potential for danger brings with it for the spouse and the family the undeniable weight of worry. In the survey conducted, 80 percent of the spouses agreed that the concern for the officer's personal safety is their number one fear, followed by the fear of the officer contracting Aids or hepatitis. A common fear is the spouse having an affair and losing the traditional family (discussed in the chapter "A Heavy Price"). The presence of weapons is another significant fear. Royal Canadian Mounted Police and Ontario Provincial Police families have the added fear of transfers. There are many concerns for both the officer and his family, some of which are more evident and easier to solve, and others which are more difficult and require professional assistance.

My worst fear was that Paul would be shot when he was stationed at 51 Division, more commonly known as 'the armpit of the police force', or 'Fort Apache'. An article dated January 1996 in *Toronto Life* states, "Geographically it is the smallest division in the city, but one of the busiest and most diverse." A place littered with ten-dollar prostitutes, crack dealers, molesters and criminals who no longer fear the police. It is not uncommon to hear gunshots being fired from the apartments behind the police station. It is an area where young couples fornicate in the street and the homeless freeze to death among the city's strangers.

Soon after Paul and I moved to 51 Division, I became emotionally and mentally drained, from worry. I slept little on the night shifts and I ate far too much. I felt the way I had when he first began working in the police department 20 years earlier. I became agitated if he was more than 15 minutes late and didn't call. I constantly worried about the late-night knock at the door, from a fellow officer bearing the bad news. I became so anxious and irritable that it began to affect our marriage. We quarreled relentlessly for ridiculous reasons or went on for days in stone-cold silence. Predictably, it also affected our sex life.

The fact that he had countless brushes with death made me crazy. I remember one particular incident when Paul worked an evening shift. It was 10:00 p.m. and he was hungry. He drove to Ed's, his favorite greasy spoon, for a quick bite. He wasn't out of the car for 10 minutes, but upon returning he heard the radio crackle and the dispatcher, in a calm voice, ask the driver of scout car 5103 to please remove himself from the vehicle and stand as far away as possible. A body of bomb squad officers wearing their dark blue tactical uniforms was already there, and carefully and thoroughly dismantled the car. A civilian had placed a call to the police station upon witnessing the culprit affixing a round object, which looked like a bomb, underneath the front of the vehicle.

I was so angry with Paul's reaction to this incident. He shrugged it off and said he was more concerned that his food was sitting on the seat getting cold. I couldn't share in his dark humor, and the fact that it wasn't really a bomb did nothing to diminish my worry.

Depending on the division, the posting in the department, the particular shift that week or just something in the news where you feel personally involved, you may be more vulnerable to fear. Many of us find that as years go by fear becomes better hidden, but it can be just as intense as ever.

When friends look at you sympathetically and ask, "How can you stand it; aren't you afraid something will happen to him?" those old fears can resurface instantly.

Dead or Delayed?

One of the most challenging fears is that of the late-night arrival. If an officer apprehends a criminal they might have hours of tedious paperwork ahead of them. Unlike workers who can set aside their work or lug it home with them, officers must complete the forms, oftentimes with the suspect sitting across from them supplying the information. The officer may be called upon to guard a crime scene and may not have access to a telephone. We wait and hope that call will come to reassure us.

Paul was on the evening shift and had apprehended a murder suspect at 2:00 a.m., only one hour before the end of his shift. I awoke with a start at 3:30, listening carefully for the familiar sounds. If it was an unusually stressful night, Paul would grab a beer and a bite and watch television. Even though this habit was aggravating, I now longed to hear those sounds. All was quiet. I sat up in bed and waited. At 3:45 a.m. I climbed out of bed and sat by the window waiting for the beam of lights from the old Honda to come around the corner of our court. At 4:00 a.m. I watched a droning real estate infomercial and then turned it off. I picked up the phone and set it down. Should

I call and risk embarrassing him again? The last time the guys mercilessly teased him—"the wifey called, wants to know if you're comin' home yet." I began reading a new book but I couldn't concentrate. I heard Michelle and Trevor stir and talk out in their sleep as if they too felt my uneasiness. At 5:30 a.m. I finally got the call. I picked up the receiver before the first ring was complete.

"Sorry I couldn't call earlier. I'll explain when I get home," he said, sounding tired and frustrated. It was just enough reassurance to allow me to fall into a deep sleep until he arrived home at 7:30 a.m.

This is a common scenario with a police officer's family. The fear of losing your spouse can cause a multitude of problems that can be unhealthy for a relationship. And families who have an officer in the drug squad or undercover have an even more demanding and troublesome lifestyle, not having any contact with their spouse for days or weeks at a time.

When Mark called from the hospital to tell me he had broken his nose and needed a few stitches to his left eye, I realized we were not like other couples. They give their spouses a kiss before leaving for work knowing where they are going and when they'll be back. I give Mark a kiss as if it were my last.

It's just the idea that on any working day the officer could be murdered. The spouse attempts to put those fears on the back burner, gives her spouse a loving goodbye and continues on with a normal working day. But as much as we like to ignore these feelings, they are always a tiger at our door.

Gene picked up his six-year-old son Peter, gave him a big hug and told him to be good for his mother while he was at work. "Okay, Dad," Peter replied. "Are you going to catch the bad guys?"

"I'm certainly going to try," laughed Gene.

"Don't tell Mom or she'll cry again when you leave," moped Peter.

Gene had no idea that his wife worried so much about him. He had never guessed that under that proud exterior there was so much pain. He decided that he would do everything in his power to come home safely so that he could hear her say how much she loved him and how proud she was to be married to a cop.

Each spouse responds differently to his or her fears. Loving reassurance can often be just enough to get by that evening.

A letter to Ann Landers:

I am a police officer's wife. As I sit in my living room watching the news on TV, I hear that two police officers have been wounded. There is no word as to the extent of the injuries or the victims' identities.

The TV shows a helicopter picking up the victims and I know it is serious. I freeze while I wait to hear the location and a numbness comes over me. Is my husband dead or alive, wounded or okay? I catch my breath and realize I must call the district. The phone number I have known for so long will not come to me now. I must calm down, take a deep breath and remember. The line is busy. What do I do now? I page my husband's beeper and leave a code number that means "Are you all right?" I try the district again. The line is still busy. I pray I don't hear a car pull up outside my house because I know that would be bad news. I finally reach someone at the district and tell him my husband works in the area of the shooting, and I need to know if he is okay. Although it seems an eternity, the man quickly answers that my husband is fine. I hang up the phone and cry. That is what it's like to be a police officer's wife.

The Ultimate Fear

As soon as she opened the door on that cold October morning and stared into the pained eyes of a police officer and a chaplain, she knew her husband was never coming home.

"When they came to my door at 3:30 a.m., part of me just died," Nancy MacDonald said. Her husband was Constable Joseph MacDonald, a five-year veteran of the Sudbury Regional Police Department who was beaten and shot. "I had told Joe to be careful that night, just as I always did."

The never-ending battle with a judicial system that gives violent criminals lenient sentences and early paroles makes officers' jobs more difficult, knowing that a life sentence doesn't usually mean 'put away for life'. Sudbury police officer Joe MacDonald was killed by two men in 1993. One of them was a convict on parole. There are many others.

Fear of the Unknown

This fear, when officers are summoned to potentially dangerous calls, can be unnerving, but we must remember that they practice caution along with intuition and experience. We must allow for open communication so that, if the officer undergoes difficulties with certain calls, he will feel free to discuss what's bothering him. By not discussing these fears and building walls to protect his spouse, the officer does not realize he is leaving the spouse to feel alone and abandoned. Open communication can help identify those fears and put them to rest so that both partners can feel safe.

Paul recalls a warm and quiet Sunday afternoon in July. He was riding with a rookie officer when they received a radio call to attend a middle-class residential area regarding 'unknown trouble'. They arrived at the address and were met at the door by several Asian women, who were frantic and unable to communicate in English.

One paced back and forth, pointing into the house, and the other was holding one hand over her face, sobbing. With the other hand she pulled Paul's arm toward the house, down the hallway to a set of stairs that led to the basement. There were 10 steps down to a small landing, where they reversed direction and continued down a few more. The woman continued to point down the stairs, yelling in her language. It was impossible to know whether there was someone sick or injured. Paul and his partner started carefully down the first few steps and noticed a young Asian male who, although short, was as wide as a garage door and was advancing upward from the second set of steps. As he reached the landing he shot Paul a crazed look and lifted a machete up over his head in a threatening motion. Paul was so surprised he backed up the stairs and tripped on his partner, who was six inches behind, pinning him to the stairs. The male advanced and Paul drew his gun, screamed, "stop or I'll shoot," and tightened his finger on the trigger. The male hesitated a second, which to Paul seemed more like an eternity, and then very slowly lowered the machete. With a blank look on his face, he turned and walked back down the stairs. The officers followed, trying to keep him in sight, and after 15 minutes of hand signals he finally put the knife down and sat on a couch.

This is a tame example of some of the tense and frightening situations these officers must deal with on a daily basis. At the back of their mind is the constant thought that one quick reaction could haunt them for a very long time. When they arrive back in the safety of their homes they feel a great weight has been lifted. It is the comfort, strength and support from their family that ensures relief and that sense of stability.

Weapons

Another very powerful concern for the spouse of an officer is the threatening presence of a gun. Weapons in the house can be intimidating. Some officers continue to wear their uniforms home, a welcome second skin to them, while we often shudder at the very sight of the gun and its capabilities.

Diane is a weapons activist and guns make her feel extremely uncomfortable. The children were not allowed to play with toy weapons or watch violence on television. She became increasingly alarmed at her husband's decision to tote his gun home from each shift. She could hear the familiar clinking of the keys in the door, the clank of his boots against the wall and the heavy rotation of the pistol as he removed each bullet. She avoided the spare-room closet where he stored the locked weapon. She watched the children every second because she had heard of an officer who had been shot with his own loaded revolver by his teenaged son. She went out of her way to keep peace in their marriage. Diane admits she lives in fear.

The officer has been highly trained in the use of weapons and treats them with the utmost respect. He does not see them as a threat, only as a severe method of protection. The spouse should ask questions and perhaps handle the revolver while it is unloaded, and watch carefully as the safety lock or handcuffs are secured into place and the gun is hidden away. If you are uncomfortable with a gun in the house, tell your spouse how you feel and ask him to leave it at work. In any case, the majority of officers prefer not to be seen in uniform on their travels home. After a 10-hour shift in uniform the anonymity is welcomed.

I had an experience with Paul's gun that I will never forget. That menacing piece of metal always troubled me. One night Paul arrived home with his new addition, a shiny black .40 caliber Glock, semi-automatic handgun that held 15 hollow point bullets. He had completed the training course with his 'new equipment' with a better-than-average score. Like an eager cowboy he demonstrated his newly learned skills. Despite the fact that he was 'playing' with a real unloaded gun, I had to laugh to myself at the intensity and serious-ness with which he pulled it out of his holster. I expected him to do his John Wayne drawl and saunter over to the kitchen sink. In good humor I offered to fashion a lasso from some tea towels. He looked a little hurt but continued to practice.

I was not prepared for what happened the following morning. The gun had been safely locked and put in his secret hiding spot. He awoke at 5:00 a.m. and we talked briefly about his day's plans. I sleepily acknowledged him, then turned to catch another hour's snooze. Minutes later a movement above my head startled me and I turned to see Paul pointing his gun directly over my stomach and lin-ing up a target. I froze in terror. Maybe he was still mad at my lasso joke.

"You wanna see it or not?" he asked, pointing to the night site at the top of his gun. He must have noticed the pallor of my skin and the delirious look in my eyes and realized what he'd done. He thought I had been lying awake and listening. That's when he decid-ed the best place for his gun was in the gun locker at work.

Officers have continual gun training courses at an indoor shooting range where they learn to hold, aim and discharge their firearms. Using a faceless body target with four large circles drawn around the central body mass, they learn judgment calls and quick reaction times.

We are constantly being reminded by family, friends and the media that the streets are becoming increasingly more dangerous. There is also a shortage of front-line officers in many of our busy cities, and this serious problem must be addressed in regards to their safety. We know that the respect once given to a police officer has now become hostility and that their authority is constantly being challenged. There are more weapons being used by criminals, and officers are forced to use their guns more often to protect the public and themselves. They must expect the unexpected. Using a firearm takes a great amount of responsibility and proficiency. The training helps an officer know when to use it and to only use it as a last resort for defense. When he makes that split-second decision he must instinctively know that there is no alternative if he is to save his own life or that of an innocent citizen.

If an officer does decide he must use a gun, the impact on the officer and his family is horrendous. The officer may blame himself when in fact there was no other choice. In some way they pay for those choices forever. In a *Toronto Star* article, Constable Mike Leone stated, "They gave me a medal. They should have given one to every member of my family."

But Take Comfort...

The officer's attire is checked by a sergeant at the beginning of each shift during parade to make certain he is wearing his mandatory bulletproof vest and carrying the equipment that will keep him safe. These officers continue to take courses in self-defense and are briefed in communication skills so that they can deal with the variety of situations presented to them each day. They are equipped with the best technology both in and out of their modes of transportation and, most importantly, they have dependable partners who loyally work alongside them. What they need most from us is tireless emotional support.

Equipped with this knowledge, never allow your imagination to get the best of you. You will be wasting precious energy. By gathering as much information about your spouse's job as you can, by listening and understanding that they are highly trained, and by trusting them—this is how you can lay your fears to rest.

The best way for me to handle my fears was to join an officer on a typically busy evening shift to see first-hand what the job entailed. This is not a good idea for the faint of heart, but despite some tense situations I gained a great respect for the officers and I felt reassured that they *do not* take any unnecessary chances.

Diseases

There is a growing concern for officers who might come in contact with hepatitis or Aids victims. People in professions that must physically deal with the public are taught to take precautionary measures. Officers wear rubber gloves in situations where they feel they might be in contact with the victim's blood. Most often this occurs at an accident scene, in a brawl or when apprehending drug addicts with dirty needles.

Paul's call from a Toronto hospital at 2:00 a.m. was not like the others where he had his nose broken, his ribs bruised or an arm slashed. This one put a real stab of fear through my heart. He had apprehended a suspect and, in searching through his pockets, Paul had pierced his hand with a dirty needle. He was given a hepatitis shot and sent home. You can imagine what went through my mind during the next few months. Any time he contracted a stubborn cold or when he looked tired or seemed restless the same frightening thought would cross my mind.

These officers must have their blood tested immediately. They are covered by Workmen's Compensation for any injury or illness on the job.

Pulling Up Roots

Relocating raises a serious fear that many police families must face. The Ontario Provincial Police, the Royal Canadian Mounted Police and Military Police can be posted far from their homes in extremely remote areas, which officers and their families would not normally consider as a choice move. It is both physically and emotionally trying for these families, who must leave their main support system of family and friends, sometimes every two or three years. The spouses feel resentment for having to uproot their children and belongings to start somewhere new. Feeling unsettled and unstable, these families must find new roots at schools, jobs and with friends. It's no wonder that moving is high on the stress list.

An R.C.M.P. wife recalls some of her moves, which brought about many changes and adjustments in her life.

There have been a number of stressful situations during this time when I felt totally alone while my husband worked, but I was also in a new community without the privilege of the previous support of my family and friends. I often felt resentful that he was given all the support and instruction and I was left to fend for myself. I constantly asked why I had allowed myself to get into this kind of lifestyle. I wondered who would look after me and my children, what could I do to keep myself busy and where could I go. I became negative and extremely depressed, which eventually led to short-term abuse of alcohol. As the wife of an officer I was unconditionally expected to cope with everything, including his absence. I became the main disciplinary figure, nurse, psychiatrist, maid and moral supporter. I came very close to a nervous breakdown.

For these families who feel they are in constant upheaval, a good sense of humor is invaluable. Working together as a family and a team can make this a positive experience. Include the children in all your moving plans. Send for brochures and maps from your nearest tourist bureau and seek interesting attractions in the area. Check out the local church and speak to the priest or pastor about volunteer work. If it's possible, load up the kids and pets and take a drive to the new area before you move in. Introduce yourself to your neighbors, sign yourself and your children up for activities offered through the town or school.

This gypsy-like existence can be fun. Make plans to visit loved ones ahead of time, perhaps for a special occasion such as Christmas or a birthday, and this will give you something to look forward to.

A very positive spouse of a military police officer said, "I always took our Gingerbread clock that had once belonged to my grandfather so that no matter where we were stationed, when I heard that old familiar dong, I knew we were home."

Helen Shields, whose husband Greg is an emergency task force officer with the R.C.M.P., states: "We've moved so often, I think our fear would be setting down roots. We love moving. It has broadened our view and made us a close family."

Diane and David remember their last bittersweet move. Their neighbors gave them a farewell party. Each person was asked to bring a special picture and place it in a photo album to be given to the couple. The neighbors asked them not to open it until they began their long trip to British Columbia the following day. With heavy hearts they flipped to the first page to see a picture of their eccentric neighbor, Doug, in female attire. Each picture brought both laughter and tears, but also great comfort in knowing they would always remain friends. When they arrived at their new home they were surprised to be greeted by friendly neighbors carrying brownies and bright wishes. Inside their empty house in the far corner of the pale blue living room, by the fireplace, floated 10 bright red balloons, and on the mantel sat a bottle of red wine with a note attached. They read, "We hope you are as happy in this house as we've been. Best of luck." It was signed by the previous owners.

If you know of any family moving to your town, remember how

difficult the adjustment must be for them, whether they work for the police services, for a company, or have moved for any other reason. Try to embrace the new neighbors by inviting them to dinner or for a casual cup of coffee. Give them as much information (excluding gossip) on the area and its people as you can. Remember that a friendly face is a real blessing.

Kids Count

Kids are the loyal and generous pieces of the police family puzzle. They perceive the world as it is and accept reality without question. I could never have asked for a more gracious and enthusiastic audience than these young people who wanted to share how they felt about being a part of a police family, no holds barred.

I Arrest Them!!

As adults we often forget that children can comprehend more then they can express, and we sometimes overlook hardships they may be encountering. Police children can experience the same worries and fears, joys and sorrows as the spouse. Parents carrying on what they believe are private discussions about police incidents are sometimes overheard by the children. What they hear and how they decipher it, especially if they are young, could become a traumatic experience.

Jamie was about seven when he overheard his Dad talking about an incident that happened at work. He was downstairs playing with his sister and we didn't hear him come to the doorway where he stood listening, frozen in horror. Norm was discussing a call with a knife-wielding criminal who had confronted him the night before. He described the complete scene in vivid detail, enacting the stabbing motions and the violent arrest that ensued. He admitted he was still a little shaken and wasn't sure how he

*survived unscathed. The picture Jamie saw in his already over-
ly active imagination must have been frightening. In fact, Jamie
suffered from nightmares for weeks.*

Paul and I received a disturbing call from Trevor's grade 2 teacher.
Trevor had become aggressive, wrestling with his schoolmates in the
playground. When we confronted Trevor about his behavior he
proudly admitted, "If they aren't being nice, I arrest them." The
teacher had also remarked that Trevor had been telling some tall tales
in the classroom about his father arresting a bad guy who had a gun
and about a lady 'puking in his car'. This was Trevor's way of dealing with stories he'd heard at home. We confessed to the teacher that
these 'stories' were in fact true accounts of incidents Paul had dealt
with at work and that Trevor must have accidentally overheard our
conversations while we thought he was watching television. This
new aggression that his teacher had detected in Trevor was a result of
hearing those stories.

Children's Fears

Discussing police work is healthy between spouses, but they must
use discretion around children. Kids are aware of some of the dangers their parents may face, but giving them vivid accounts of police
incidents will only cause them needless worries and fears.

One of the greatest fears any child will suffer is that they might
lose a parent, either to violence, to sickness or to the ever-so-devas-
tating break-up. In a police family that fear may be more prominent.
In the survey, police kids from ages 10 to 25, when asked what their
greatest fear was about their parent being an officer, all agreed it was
the fear that their parent might be killed in the line of duty. Watching
television programs where officers spend the majority of their time
killing people or being killed, listening to the news, reading the paper

and listening to stories at home provide genuine reasons for feeling that fear.

Fearful kids can become mentally and physically anxious. Those concerns can manifest themselves in behavioral problems at home, nightmares or disciplinary problems at school. They can suffer the same physical symptoms as an adult—loss of appetite, stomach problems, headaches and sleeplessness.

Unlike adults, children do not have a well-developed ability to control their fears. Parents must recognize their concerns and reassure them by conveying to the child that the officer is very knowledgeable in how to protect himself and the public. They need to use the wisdom they've painstakingly acquired over the years to assist that child. One mother eased her child's fear by no longer allowing him to watch violent television programs, especially police-related ones, and refrained from discussing any negative police incidents around him.

I told Mark that Daddy had a hard job to do but that God always looked after him. Each evening Mark repeated the same prayer, "...and, God, please look after my dad while he's looking after everybody else."

There are children who have been unfortunate enough to have suffered the terrible loss of a police parent. They eventually realize, either on their own or with professional help, that their parent died honorably by helping and protecting others. No parents wish their children to experience this kind of anguish, and they feel powerless to control the anxious feelings their children may be confronting.

From the *CPA Express* magazine for police officers, summer 1996:

"You were my hero, Dad. You will always be my hero," said Patrick Lalonde, 22. Lalonde wore his father's kepi as the casket was taken away from the church. An equally heart-wrenching sight occurred moments later when Patrick's sister Nathalie, 28, hugged the coffin and cried until pallbearers reached the hearse. She was helped to a waiting car by her brother.

"He's Never Home"

When interviewing teenagers I asked what they didn't like about their police parent's career choice. Besides fear, shift work was a major complaint. One 12-year-old enjoys wrestling and playing floor hockey with his friends when they come to visit.

He's never home and when he is he's sleeping. I gotta be careful not to wake him up. I hate telling everyone they have to be quiet or that they can't play at my house 'cause my dad's sleeping.

One patrol officer's 13-year-old said that the only problem with the shift work was that he couldn't crank up the music because his dad was sleeping. For Christmas last year his dad received a wireless headset so that he could watch television on a late shift, but it didn't take long for the 13-year-old to claim it. Now it's his mother's yelling for him that wakes up his dad. You can't win!

Children going to school may not see the parent for days and sometimes weeks at a time. When they finally get a chance to spend some time, it could be when Dad's in a sleepy stupor at the dinner table or maybe on a trip to the bathroom at 3:00 a.m. when he's just getting home, or during a rushed breakfast when he's arrived after a night shift, totally drained.

In times such as these, the spouse and her children are brought together to form a closer bond. Brothers and sisters seek comfort in each other's company, sharing the common emptiness of a missing parent, and lean on each other and the remaining parent who is trying to fill both shoes. When kids start feeling sorry for themselves they need to be reminded that there are many families who have a parent with a career that entails a great amount of traveling and some who don't have the wonderful privilege of a second parent, or any parents.

It was the last game in the playoffs and we were tied 2-2 and I was playing goalie. We played really hard all season. I didn't want to let my team down. I looked for my mom and my brother in the stands and saw them give the good luck thumbs up. The guys on the other team were bigger and their goalie was better then me, but I was going to try my best. The puck kept coming at me and I managed to keep most of them out. I saved a really good one but then there was a rebound shot, and I stretched all the way out and saved it again. We won! The whole team skated to me and that's when I saw my dad and his partner with their noses against the glass, waving. It was the most exciting game I'd ever played because my dad was there to see me make the final save.

The 16-year-old son of a staff sergeant admitted that he was 'really pissed' his dad couldn't come to many of his games or special events.

I don't care now but when I was little I remember all the dads would show up for the soccer games to support their kids and because my mom didn't drive and my dad was always working I had to catch a ride with someone else. I kinda felt alone. I was really pissed at my dad because he wasn't there when I really needed him, like when this guy at school punched me in the face and I ran all the way home and the one person I wanted to talk to most wasn't there again. He never made it to my grade 8 graduation either. I guess it's not his fault but I feel I got the dirty end of the stick.

But when I asked him if he remembered any fond memories with his dad it didn't take long for him to shoot me a huge metal smile and say, "Oh yeah, I remember when..." and continue to recount some exciting stories of times he'd shared with his father.

Some kids are fortunate enough to have a police parent who works in the district in which they live and can attend some of the kid's school and sports events, and can even come home for lunch. The kids are quite happy when their police parent drives up in a patrol car, dressed in uniform, perhaps with their partner, just to say hello.

Ingrid Ester has been with the police department for 17 years and has four children, ages 5 to 14.

Rebecca had her grade 4 Christmas recital. I told her I would be working but that her dad and grandma would be there with her. She was really disappointed but gave me a brave smile, which just about broke my heart. She was playing the lead part of Mother Mary and was kneeling over Baby Jesus when I walked into the gym. It didn't take long for her to spot me and she was so surprised she dropped the baby to wave and yell, "Hey, Mom, over here!" The whole gym turned to look at me.

It really bothers me that I've missed some of the special times but I try to make up for it when I'm home by doing something special with them. They're really pretty good about it.

A Moving Lifestyle

In the interviews with young people of all ages I was happy to find that they all expressed a great amount of pride in their parent's choice of career despite some of the difficulties they encounter. One of these difficulties is the frequent moving.

Fourteen-year-old Marco Soave's father is with the Royal Canadian Mounted Police and is posted in countries all over the world.

I was really lucky because I got to travel and meet a lot of new friends. The hardest part is always moving away.

Children of police officers who move on a regular basis don't always adapt as well as adults. Some find that they are afraid to become immersed in a friendship because it will hurt too much when they leave. This causes them to build a defensive wall, not allowing people to get close. Some kids, like Marco, see moving as a wonderful experience. He has no problems meeting new people because he continues to maintain those friendships despite the distance. Marco's mother tells me that her son calls people in all the countries he's lived. "You never know when we'll go back," she said.

Discipline

At times it seems as if the officer is only home long enough to be the disciplinarian. The kids think he's overprotective and too strict. Parents find they end up arguing about the other's method of disciplining. The officer deals with the problem by taking immediate action, usually taking a cop's view before thinking it through, and suddenly the spouse finds she becomes protective and takes the side of the child.

Because officers are used to being in complete control at work, when they use the same technique at home they are shocked to find they are usually unsuccessful. Kids, especially teenagers, do not like to be treated unfairly or without respect and will immediately rebel.

This becomes a vicious circle—parent takes control, child gets back up, parent becomes frustrated and more determined to make the child listen, child rebels and can cause problems in other areas. Then it starts again with the next incident.

Parents protect and guide their children to keep them safe from harm, not realizing that trying to control a teenager at a time when he's attempting to develop an identity of his own can be problematic. Enforcing strict rules and regulations makes for a good police officer, but using that same tactic on a teenager can cause major waves. Kids want parents who are fair and treat them with respect. They want to learn by experimentation and need to learn on their own that mistakes have consequences. They want to spread their wings and get a taste of being their own person and not be overprotected. As with any family raising teenagers, you learn to give children the tools of decent values and morals in the hope they will use them as they get older.

Michael was 14 at the time. His father had asked him to take the garbage out but like most teens, he forgot. The next day, after the disposal trucks had come and gone, Ken came home furious. "I asked you twice in two weeks and you forgot both times," he yelled at Michael, who was engaged in the complex job of putting together the new stereo system he got for his birthday. "Get that garbage together now and put it in the car. We'll drive it over to a dumpster," Ken demanded. Michael told him that he'd do it later when he was finished. "No, this minute." Ken lost complete control, marched over to the system and pulled out the plugs, taking one of the pieces of equipment. He then gave Michael a long lecture, accusing him of being lazy and commanding him to go and get the garbage and put it in the car. Ken's stance and his voice made Michael feel he was nothing more then a criminal. That's what really hurt.

"My Dad's a Cop"

When teachers, neighbors and other children ask police kids about their parent, the 'cop kids' sometimes begin to feel their family is different from others, especially if they have been teased by their peers. Some kids decide at an early age that it's better not to disclose their parent's career, and can become clever at changing the subject.

Trevor started as early as eight to recognize that his dad held a job that provoked different responses from his classmates and friends. Once when the teacher asked her students to draw a picture of their dad at work, Trevor drew Paul carrying a bag of salt over his shoulder. At the time we were managing our own small salt business. Curious and a little hurt, Paul asked if Trevor knew what he did at work and Trevor happily responded, "Yeah, you're a policeman." He was very proud of his father's choice of career; he just wasn't interested in dealing with the response from other kids. Kids listen to other parents talk, and occasionally a parent receives a ticket and so has nothing positive to say about police.

Some kids find that using their parent's position as an officer to conveniently protect themselves can cause added problems, especially if the ruffian thinks the police child is using it as a shield. Any teen who's been in trouble with the police might take advantage of the situation and take his anger out on the officer's child. Often enough peers will refer to a police kid as a "goody, goody," which may either cause the fists to fly or bring on a feeling of alienation from other kids.

Daniel, aged 17, was wearing the new expensive leather sports jacket he had received for Christmas. On his way home a couple of teens from another school demanded the jacket and threatened to beat him up. Daniel was nervous and thought the only way he'd be able to make his escape was by telling them his dad was a cop, who would come after them if they tried anything. A couple of gang members called him a few names and had the good sense to leave, but it was the scruffiest of the four that remained and demanded the jacket again. When Daniel refused and turned to run, the troublemaker grabbed the jacket, giving Daniel a good kick in the groin. As he ran off he yelled back, "Tell your old man to come looking for me, I'll be waiting!" Afraid that this bully might hurt his father, he told his parents he'd left the jacket somewhere and when he went back to look for it, it was gone.

Liz's husband Lorne works for the Toronto Police Service.

My daughter had problems when certain kids found out that her father was a cop. They teased her and needled her constantly. Depending on the area in which you live, kids may encounter difficulties, so sometimes it's better they remain silent.

A sergeant with the Ontario Provincial Police, stationed in a small northern town in Ontario, fears for his children.

We've had a couple of incidents where criminals know where the officer lives and have terrorized the family. I had our phone number unlisted because someone continued to call and harass my wife and kids. It can be really scary when it involves your own family especially when you're working shifts.

Many of the teens I spoke to prefer not to discuss their police parent's career. In the high school years when kids are at a defiant age, telling someone that their parent is a cop may only fuel the fire and make things more difficult, so that they might be subjected to more taunting. Children in elementary school are no exception; they must deal with extremely cruel mocking in the confines of the playground.

Parents need to cultivate a sense of pride in their children from an early age so that they appreciate what their parents do, whether it be a police officer or a homemaker, bestowing upon them a strong sense of self that will protect them from the adverse public and media attacks.

Nikki has been with the police department for eight years.

When asked what his mother did, my five-year-old happily replied, "She bakes cakes and drives a police car." He really loves cake. But he is especially proud of his mommy being a police officer. He always wants to try on my uniform and runs through the house blowing the whistle. He sees me both as a homemaker and as a police officer and likes both equally well.

Paul and I have been lucky to have kids whose good friends have shown a great amount of respect and interest in Paul's job. They ask questions about his uniform and his gun and listen to his stories with genuine curiosity. It's a world they know little about and find intriguing. Some young adults have gone one step further, to seek added information about the hiring process of the job and offer themselves as volunteers.

'Cop Kids' and the Law

Police officers often expect more from their children than other families, especially when it comes to obeying the law. This expectation can cause children to rebel just to prove that they are individuals who have different values and attitudes from their police parents. They are aware that the officer deals with criminal elements every day and that his reaction to bad behavior is due to others' behaviors. Many kids talked about feeling constricted, being on a leash, and feeling that their other friends had more freedom so once again they were made to feel different.

One officer revealed that his children, who are 17 and 13, still think he'll lose his job if they break the law:

I told them that if they get into trouble I could lose my job. I've been telling them that for years and if it works, why not. A little fear never hurt anyone; this way they'll stop and think before they jump into something inappropriate.

Brad Watson, whose mother Marlene is a staff inspector with Toronto Police, advises police children:

Don't get into any trouble or you'll get it twice. First when you get caught by the police and then you get it again from your police parent when you get home. Just be careful, they probably won't be fired but it could hurt or ruin their reputation.

Brad was young when his mother was a patrol officer. She was one of the first to go on maternity leave.

People find it shocking when I tell them that it's my mom who's a cop, especially when they find out she's a staff inspector. I'm really proud of her and I would like to follow in her footsteps.

One police officer who works for a police department in a small town had asked police officers in the station to give his son a ticket if they caught him speeding. His son seemed to think that because he held his dad's card and everyone knew him that he could get away with anything. It didn't take long for him to get his first ticket.

He was shocked when he came home to tell me that he'd gotten a ticket. He figured he'd never have a problem. I didn't tell him that I knew and that I'd arranged for the guys to keep an eye on him because I knew he was heavy-footed. It was a good lesson.

In His Footsteps

The survey asked spouses for their reaction to their children showing interest in becoming police officers, and 80 percent said they would not interfere but would make other suggestions, especially those who had daughters who seemed interested. Twenty percent said they had no problem with the choice and would support them without interfering.

Ever since Adam was four he wanted to be a policeman like his dad. I never let him see my negative feelings about it. I felt if I did, I'd be criticizing the very career that his dad dedicated himself to and our source of livelihood. But I really would rather he chose another career because I know I would be worried sick about him. Now he's 17 and he's thinking about volunteering as an auxiliary police. What can I do but support him?

Randy has just been accepted by the police department in Saskatchewan.

I'm really excited because it's all I've ever wanted. Both my parents are cops and they love what they do and they're really good at it. That's why I couldn't understand why they kept trying to talk me out of it. I know they're proud of me, I could tell at the ceremonies, but I guess they worry 'cause they really know what it's like out there.

One mother threw her arms up during an interview and expressed her disappointment.

I don't want him to get into the same line of work. I have enough on my mind worrying about his father, but it would kill me if anything happened to Brian. He's heard all the stories from his dad

and they must have had an impact on him. I even told Brian we'd
pay for a trip to Europe if he'd reconsider, but his mind was set.

Tips from the Kids

Marco Soave offers some advice for kids:

Respect your parent for who he is both as a parent and a police
officer. If he's had a bad day take the time to sit down and talk
to him and try to cheer him up. That's what I try to do whenev-
er my dad's having a hard day.

Marco feels that living in a police lifestyle is exciting and very
'normal' to him.

When my dad is home he is a great protector. He's like an alarm.
Where most people panic in emergency situations, my dad knows
exactly what to do. He loves the job he does and I love him for
who he is.

Twin brothers Colin and Shawn Venables, 15-year-olds, agree that
they find they really appreciate their father and worry that one day he
might not come home.

I wish he didn't have to work on holidays and special days but I
know he has to be out there protecting the public. Be proud of
him and support him; he's doing a great job out there.

A Personal Note

In writing this chapter and listening to many kids, all of whom were
very proud to have police parents, I just assumed that our children

had never had any problems with their lifestyle. I was wrong and totally surprised that one did and one didn't.

Michelle, at age 19, admits that she has had some difficult times keeping aloof during controversial conversations with other teenagers at school, at work or at the bar scene when they made derogatory comments about police officers. "They just don't understand what they really do out there," she said. "They don't see the whole picture and it makes me so frustrated when I can't explain some of the things we go through with him at home."

Michelle also admitted that she worries fretfully about her dad. "I remember it was around grade 5 or 6 when I started having nightmares about Dad getting hurt. I think it was after he came home with a broken nose and ribs from a fight at work. I didn't want to tell my parents about the nightmares in case it worried them."

Living this lifestyle has made her more sensitive to people's moods. She can sense when her dad is approachable and when he needs his space. "I can always tell by Dad's body language if he's had a bad day and I know to stay away until I see he's settled down. I try changing the subject when I see he's ready to argue and try making him laugh."

Our son Trevor, at 15, is very relaxed about his dad's career and how it affects our home. He has never been concerned about his dad's time away or his working holidays. The shifts don't bother him, although he agrees with his sister that Dad can be a "mean dude if he doesn't get his sleep."

He does remember "when Dad used to come on my school trips when all the other dads were working. He would tell the kids funny stories that happened at work and they all loved him."

Trevor doesn't worry like his sister because he knows his dad can handle himself and that he always has a partner or a backup. "There's only one thing that really bothers me," he says, "and that's when some parents tell their kids that the policeman will take them to jail if they don't behave. Those parents are just teaching their children to be afraid of the people who might help them one day."

To Sum Up...

Most young people have thought about the possibilities of their parents being hurt on the job but as they get older they've learned to acknowledge it and put it aside. It only comes to the surface if they see a police officer hurt or killed on television or on the news, or someone brings it up.

Citizens who don't understand the police lifestyle have told their children not to become involved with or marry a police officer because it entails certain dangers. What they don't think about is that even though officers can be at risk, there are other jobs that are just as dangerous, if not more so. Norma and Darien have one such job.

My husband and I work as window washers in Toronto. We have our own business and we are always busy. I couldn't count the number of times that we've had close calls climbing up and down those towering buildings. Actually Darien has fallen twice and had both his legs and one arm broken.

The more positive side of being a 'cop kid' is having the opportunity to learn interesting aspects of the law. The child becomes more aware of what problems face society and what difficulties confront police, judges and politicians. He or she learns that their police parent is doing a job that helps people and in turn improves the society in which they live. They see that the parent is committed to a job where he continues to enforce the law despite the negative opinions from the public and the media, and he extends that same behavior to enforce the more traditional values in the home. Even if at times the parent seems too overprotective or too controlling, kids learn that he is only trying to maintain that basic moral code that he passes along to his family, so that they may acquire a sense of pride and consistency in an ever-changing society.

Parenting thus becomes a balancing act for both parents, who are trying to develop good communication with their children. The majority of kids that I spoke to were bright, clean-cut, well-adjusted people with clear ambitions and goals and a great regard for human nature.

Below is a loving poem sent by Michael Davis Jr., aged eight.

My dad is a police officer
He looks really big and mean
But when he picks me high up
And I look under his hat
I see his smiling eyes
And I know he's the best.

I Smell Bacon

In the first few years of a police officer's career he begins to develop an 'us versus them' attitude, feeling that society is repeatedly attempting to outwit or outsmart him. This forces him to only trust and depend on other officers who share his view of how the world 'really is'. He develops friendships that are rooted in a mutual sharing of intense experiences during the course of his career, experiences that he knows the public could never understand.

It is sometimes necessary for officers to make quick decisions when they cannot stop to reflect or refer to a training manual and must act on the basis of their experience. They act solely on gut instinct and rely on their partner for safety and protection. These men and women who work side by side in a world that seems black and white develop a strong unbreakable bond. Even when there are personal differences, there is a fierce loyalty toward each other. They begin forming an invisible division between themselves and the rest of the world, commonly known as the 'blue wall' or 'blue line'. One officer describes the relationship with his fellow colleagues as a "marriage, till death do us part."

As a protective device from public and media criticism and scrutiny, officers retreat from the rest of society into what has been labeled as 'the brotherhood', a type of elite club where no amount of money or prestige can force entry. This is where they are most accepted because they feel no one understands them to be like other people. They possess an extraordinary shoulder-to-shoulder, heart-to-heart bond that, as outsiders, we could never fathom.

One of the major complaints from officers and their families are the vicious comments and articles written and printed by the press. Officers feel that the public is forced to view them in a negative light. Not often are the articles about police positive ones—only when they do something 'heroic'.

Both the media and the public have high expectations of police officers, but what they don't realize is that they too can make mistakes and that they are only human. They are sometimes perceived as possessing cold, distant or 'superhuman' qualities, but this is a tactic they use to hide their personal feelings. Some citizens look to officers as a symbol of society and some see them as a kind of distinct irritation, which is an attitude that further forces them to withdraw into their 'brotherhood'.

When spouses were asked in the survey how they felt about the media they agreed that the newspapers take a negative position toward police and do not deliver the proper message to their readers. There is inevitably front page coverage on any officer who makes a mistake. This causes every officer to feel he's being put on trial. The survey also asked how spouses felt society viewed police officers.

The 'silent majority' appreciates them, politicians see them as scapegoats, with our laws currently being 'toothless', and I imagine the criminal element sees them somewhere between a nuisance and a big joke.

Officers' families who have had the misfortune of a loved one caught in the clutches of the media can suffer terrible repercussions, and there is no mercy for those who have climbed the ranks to become a sitting duck for the media's scathing comments.

It affects all ages. Our daughter, who is 30, still has a really hard time when she reads about her dad in the newspaper. She doesn't understand why he always comes out looking like the 'bad guy'. She can't read it any more because she gets so upset it actually makes her physically ill.

Establishing a 'hero' column in the local newspaper that would provide daily or weekly experiences of police officers, firefighters, security, ambulance workers and nurses would allow the public to understand the kinds of demanding tasks that these professions deal with and would like to be acknowledged for.

Gone is the 'Clint Eastwood' mentality of what a cop is. Police families are happy to see true-life police programs that give the viewer a good perspective on what really happens on the beat. Screening is advisable for young children, however, especially those of an officer. The language, the nudity and the stark reality of the job can cause them needless worry.

Public Image

The public's scrutiny is not fixed solely on officers, but on their families as well. Almost always when a spouse is asked what her husband does as a career, the answer produces a pause and a stare, one of obvious curiosity or even blatant hostility. Some spouses have personally encountered people who, due to a bad experience, have cast unbelievably harsh insults. Comments that are cruel and uncalled-for put the spouse in the uncomfortable position of ferociously protecting her spouse and the honor of every police officer. The spouse quickly learns to adapt her police spouse's skill of controlling one's emotions when she hears discourteous comments such as 'pig', 'copper', 'flatfoot', 'donut boy', or 'I smell bacon, oink, oink'.

A spouse never knows when she'll encounter a citizen's outspoken opinions. No place is above reproach—at work, in the grocery store, at parties, showers, weddings and even funerals—it makes no difference. When the word 'cop' is spoken, there's always someone who feels compelled to make a comment. The best position for a spouse to take is to just to ignore it.

By answering with diplomacy or not commenting at all and demonstrating confidence and compassion, the spouse can do more to improve the police image then by being argumentative or scornful.

Police politics is a favorite topic of conversation, depending on what's 'hot' with the media at the time. These complicated matters, if not handled discreetly, can become vicious gossip that can only do the police department harm.

I was standing at a farmer's fruit stand 20 miles outside our town when I overheard two women in a heated discussion over the recent media attention on police chases. One brutally criticized police for their unprofessional manner in dealing with the incident and the other, fueled by her friend's agitation, began cursing police, bringing up every negative incident she'd ever heard about or experienced. It was really hard for me to stand and listen to their abusive lashing but I sucked in my stomach, pushed back my shoulders, picked up my corn and left. That took more backbone than you can possibly imagine.

A police family will intuitively learn when they want to be identified with law enforcement officers and when they prefer to be left unknown. Their discretion is important for the reputation of an officer, the police department and their own peace of mind.

What really annoys me is when we go where no one knows that Tony is a cop and we have to sit and listen to the attacks made on police. I get so upset I have to leave or I'm afraid I'll sock someone. Especially when I hear remarks like "where's a cop when you need one, wish I had a job where you had all that time off" and, of course, the most common one, "why don't they look for the real criminals instead of wasting their time on the little guys like us." Tony just sits and takes it; he's used to it.

Despite all the negativity over police, in a recent international survey people were asked if they thought their police did a good job. The results were astounding. Eighty percent of Canadians, the highest among all countries, said yes. The United States was a close second, with a rate of 77 percent.

In the 1997 Police Association of Ontario yearbook, an article on police and public opinion revealed the results of a public opinion poll on "The Image of Police Officers."

Respondents expressed very strong agreement with the following points of view, 10 being the strongest and most positive.
- When you become a police officer, you have to accept that you are risking your life on a daily basis. (8.9)
- Given the danger and responsibility in their jobs, police officers earn every penny they are paid. (8.4)
- If you're a police officer, you should be able to take off your uniform at the end of the day and be able to lead a private life that is separate from your professional life. (8.1)

Respondents expressed strong agreement with the following statements:
- When I walk down the street and I see a police officer, I feel safe and secure. (7.9)
- People who have police officers as spouses worry every time the phone rings. (7.6)
- Most police officers chose their profession rather than a less risky career because of their dedication to keeping the public and communities safe. (7.1)

- I would rather be married to a teacher than a police officer, because of the stresses and dangers police officers face on a daily basis. (7.1)

This is proof that citizens do understand the burdens of police work and the police lifestyle and are sympathetic to its problems.

As Police Constable Guy Woolhead from 53 Division of Toronto Police Service said in the August issue of the *News and Views* police magazine:

On Monday, May 27, 1996, I had to do something I hope I'll never have to do again. I had to shoot someone who was trying to kill me....I have a lot to be thankful for and a lot of people to thank. I'm very thankful for the four civilian witnesses who came forward and helped with the investigation.

Most civilians are aware that the police are trying to do the best job they can and when the 'chips are down', they have come forward to lend a helping hand even in situations where they might be risking their own lives.

Whenever I see a cop directing traffic on a street corner in the winter, I always stop to buy him a coffee. It's my way of saying thank you for doing a good job. I appreciate living in a neighborhood where I and my family can feel safe.

A letter sent in by Joseph Verdirame to the Toronto *Star*, dated August 8, 1998, passionately states "...let's stop being armchair cops and let the professionals do their job. I, for one, am thankful for our police officers, and I'm quite content to let them do their job."

There are days set aside in recognition of different professions and people—why not a special day for members of special services such as police, fire, ambulance and nurses, so that their dedication and hard work can be appreciated? After all, how safe would we feel without them? Who would watch over us?

The public is genuinely interested and curious about the lifestyle of a police officer, and most ask reasonable questions. There are, however, those who are not quite so diplomatic.

You get tired of people asking you the same questions. It never fails, when someone knows my husband is a cop, they always ask me if I'm worried about him getting killed. I never really know how to answer that because sometimes I'm more worried than others and sometimes I don't think about it unless someone asks. You wouldn't believe some of the questions we get.

Here are some of the most common questions asked about police, as given by their spouses in the survey:
1. Don't you worry about him being killed?
2. Has he ever used a gun on anyone?
3. Does he walk around with it loaded?
4. Does he ever drink before he goes to work?
5. Is it true that cops have a lot more opportunities to have affairs?
6. Does he ever get nervous at a call?
7. Doesn't he get tired of playing God all the time?
8. Do cops really drink a lot of coffee and eat donuts?
9. Why don't they go after the real criminals instead of giving out tickets?
10. Do they have to meet quotas?
11. Can they fix tickets?
12. Don't you get lonely?
13. Don't you get tired of having him home all the time?

In an editorial to *The Era-Banner* dated September 19, 1996, J. Elliott of the York Regional Police Service describes the kinds of pressures put on police:

> As a police officer, I am more aware that my duties don't end when I remove my uniform and go home to my family. I am held more accountable for my actions, whether on or off duty, because of my training and knowledge of the laws which I enforce. As police officers, we must always attempt to maintain the trust of the general public and be accountable for our actions.

Some spouses find that problems with the public and the media are secondary in comparison to the attacks they undergo from members of their own family.

> *They always hassle me if John can't make it to a family function. He has missed a number of celebrations over the years, and I think they've emotionally excluded him from the family. They resent the fact they can't depend on him to be there. They haven't considered how badly he feels missing out and how I feel not having him with me to share the family time together. I get so tired of those 'didn't make it again, eh?' looks.*

Families and friends need to be more aware of the difficulties in a police lifestyle and need to learn how to support both the officer and the family. Negative comments about their choice of career, shift work and duties can only add to the mountain of stresses they must already endure.

We have been extremely lucky to have both families' support. They have gone to great pains to accommodate Paul's schedule so that we can be together. If Paul is not able to attend they demonstrate their loving disappointment and turn their attention on us to make us feel special, not 'different'. In this lifestyle that is truly a great treat.

Family and friends demonstrating their loving support with kind words of encouragement can be the backbone of support to a law enforcement family.

One dear cousin, Nevis, called the day after Bill Hancox, a Toronto Police officer, was killed. "Hi," she said softly. "How are you?" I sensed a quietness, almost a shyness, in her voice. "I'm really sorry about what happened," she said with great compassion. A lump formed at the back of my throat and sat heavy and fat so I couldn't speak. "I just want you to know that we've been thinking of you," she continued. "If you need to talk, just call." That was it, short but extremely supportive and sincere at a time when we needed it most.

One police spouse wants his identity protected, and is currently having difficulty adjusting to his wife's choice of career.

Kelly was at a call where people were fighting with knives. When she and her partner tried to stop the attack she received minor cuts to her upper arm. One of the victims had been critically stabbed in the chest and died on the way to the hospital. The incident was televised and I immediately began getting calls asking if Kelly was all right. She had already called and I reassured them she was O.K. I could never describe the emotional impact that those kinds of incidents have on a family. I have a hard time with all this stuff; after all I'm the one who's supposed to protect her and I feel so useless when I can't.

A law enforcement couple must educate their family and friends by providing them with literature and discussing their unique concerns so that they understand the hardships of their lifestyle. Some people do recognize the problems but are not sure how to deal with them. Let them know it can be as easy as picking up the phone.

One spouse who was fed up with the criticism that police and families received sent a letter to the editor of the *News and Views* police magazine, dated February 1982. It reads:

To Whom It May Concern

Where are you when the alarm sounds at four in the morning and he drags his tired body out of bed?

Where are you with your comforting words when he's three hours late coming home from work because he has been injured protecting your community?

Where are you when I'm alone on my birthday, our anniversary or Christmas?

Where are you when he's working and my heart flips over because I have just heard "a policeman has been shot tonight"?

Where are you when someone spits in his face or yells obscenities in his ear?

Where are you when a drunk driver has killed a small child?

Where are you when a family outing has to be postponed because he has to go to court on his day off?

Where are you when a lonely senior citizen needs someone to talk to or help carrying groceries?

Where are you when the drug pusher he has worked so hard to catch is let off on a technicality?

Where are you when he has to notify a mother of her son's death in a traffic accident?

Where are you when his partner has been shot and he has his hands full keeping them both alive?

Where are you when he has to make a split-second decision between his life or a stranger's when confronted with a knife or a gun?

I know where you are!

You're sitting back waiting and watching for your chance to

criticize—to point out all of the mistakes—made by a human being constantly working under pressure.

You're sitting back waiting for a slip of the tongue comment made by a human being in a heated dispute.

You're sitting back waiting to yell 'police brutality' or 'discrimination' when a human being is asked to step into a domestic dispute that has gotten out of hand.

You're sitting back demanding a Citizen's Review Board to investigate Police Actions that you couldn't possibly even begin to understand—because you're not there.

When will you so-called 'critics' realize that a Police Officer is as human as you or I. He bleeds when he is cut and he cries when he hurts. He deals day-in and day-out with personalities and situations that the majority of us will never have to encounter in a whole lifetime and is very rarely told "well-done" or "have a nice day."

Well, I'm there when he comes home from work.

I'm there to make him feel important, to feed him and to hold him.

I'm there to tell him he's terrific.

I'm there to love him.

Therefore, I feel I have the right to say—"Back-off! He's doing one hell-of-a-job!"

PC's Friend—1 Traffic
(Author unknown)

Human Beings Too

To cultivate a better rapport with the public, many police departments now have a Community Policing Program. This approach places officers out in the community to talk to and deal with the public, listen to their concerns and assist in helping put those concerns to rest.

Among other reasons, it was created to help the public realize that police are human, committed and willing to communicate on a more relaxed level and to find police more approachable and understanding. A close neighbor expressed his feeling about police work: "They couldn't pay me enough to do a cop's job."

Police have chosen a career where they reap the benefits of personal satisfaction in helping society. Their valiant daily tasks may always seem to reap negative responses but they wait for that one positive one that makes the job worthwhile. As one officer put it, "Even though you never know what might happen out there and the pay's no hell, I still wouldn't change jobs with anyone."

Of the many officers I have spoken with over the years, the majority feel very passionately about their work. They are willing to risk their lives to enforce the law.

Paul asked his brother Derek to join him on a ride-along. It happened to be a busy summer night, with a full moon, and they had more action than they could handle. Racing from call to call the entire evening, they arrived home at 8:00 a.m. charged, ready not for sleep but for a few beer. As Derek put it, "I never thought it would be like this. It'll be an experience I'll never forget." Certainly not one he's ever stopped talking about.

No Money, Honey!

Police families have found that being in a trusted profession they are looked upon favorably by banks for credit (who could be more honest?). This generosity finds many families overextending themselves.

Those who have come to the mutual decision that the spouse stay at home to raise the family may find they must financially compensate by working extra time, taking paid duties (off-duty jobs) or creating businesses of their own. Officers who work rotating shifts with a number of days off find they are able to enjoy another form of employment and the extra cash. This also helps them feel more like 'normal' people.

Different departments have different rules for officers interested in other employment. Some ask the officer to complete a form requesting permission and, once it is reviewed, a decision can be made based on the amount of time committed and the choice of work.

Two officers in a large suburban town became partners in a small pub without the permission of their department. They knew they should refrain from being involved in anything that might conflict with police work. In the first week of the new bar opening, three teens, under age and under the influence, were apprehended. The officers were asked to "cease and desist."

All families find that overextending themselves both financially and physically adds more pressure, but with an officer it adds stress to an already burdened lifestyle.

Phil started his own landscaping business two years ago. He worked long hours at the department, then worked at the business day in and day out until the season was over. It was nice to have the money, but whenever we did see him he was too tired to spend time with us. The worst thing was that he had a hard time getting through his shifts and I was always afraid that if he wasn't alert something might happen to him.

One Job or Two?

In our society where the living style has become more materialistic and expensive, many couples find they both need to work. Unfortunately, in a police marriage there are distinctive problems that must be considered before that kind of decision is made. Great consideration must be given to those extra pressures that will be put on the family. Many spouses feel that the choice to stay at home is difficult but necessary. They act as the main pillar of the family and as the painter, doctor, taxi, cook, parent, etc., while their police spouse works long hours.

Helen Chambers who has been married for 45 years to Bill Chambers, a staff sergeant with Toronto Police, remembers a time when the wives of police officers didn't work.

We were needed to keep the 'home fires burning'. I never worked until the girls started school. It was too difficult with the shift work, court duties and all the extra time Bill had to work. Being a police wife is not an easy job, but being a police wife who also works outside the home can be really hard on a family.

Another police wife talks about her sacrifice:

I worked as an executive for a large company and made twice

Mark's salary with great benefits and added bonuses. We had two children and a nanny to help out but we still found it hard to spend time together. With Mark's shifts and me working six days a week and late hours we couldn't even find time for the kids. One night when I was home, Joshua, our three-year-old, wasn't feeling well and refused to let me comfort him; instead he cried for his nanny. That's when I knew I'd better do something. I couldn't ask Mark to leave his job when I knew how much he loved it. It was a really big decision but I told the company I had to leave. Luckily I was able to work part time from home. The adjustment was challenging but the payoffs were great. I think if I hadn't done it we wouldn't be together now. We have less money but no regrets.

In 1976 Paul and I bought our first home and shortly after we had our first child. Everything happened at once—the weight of financial burdens, parenting responsibilities and Paul's acceptance into the police service. The pay would be modest compared to his previous job but we both decided I should remain at home to raise a family. It didn't take long to realize that one salary wouldn't be enough. I began searching for a job where I could work around Paul's shifts. There were not many sympathetic employers; one, however, offered a waitressing position promising the hours I needed. The pay was minimum wage but the tips were good. It kept me in shape, got me out and meeting people, helped pay the bills and looked after the babysitting problem. It wasn't the kind of career I imagined, but that had to be put on hold for a few years. In the meantime it allowed us the great pleasure of raising two beautiful children.

Jaan Schaer at the Employee Assistance Program for Toronto Police Service suggests that officers and their families see a financial advisor at the beginning of their marriage. "It may seem costly but it should be the first investment every couple makes," he advises.

Long-term financial planning assists in providing the couple with a concrete feeling of security, thus eliminating what marriage counselors consider the downfall of many marriages—poor money managing.

Values and Money

Financial problems have been the cause of ruin in many relationships. There are officers who start out by 'saving the world' but somewhere down the line their aim shifts from police work to making more money. Every job has its temptations and police work is no exception.

Even small gratuities can be misconstrued as 'an unethical choice'. This is a time when officers must demonstrate the tight fabric of their strong moral code. Officers who are implicated for any crime are not well looked upon by society, media, the department or their peers. A simple 'no' is a short but powerful response. When values begin changing at work they will affect the values at home, and vice versa.

Mark and his partner drove by the same buildings each evening checking for suspicious people or illegal activity. One jewelry store in particular had been broken into a number of times. The owner offered each of the officers a piece of jewelry for their wives. They knew that it was just a tactic to get them to pay special attention to his store. They politely refused the offer but assured the owner they would pass by as often as possible.

There is a very fine line between a criminal and a cop. We sometimes have to think like them to understand what their next move might be but that doesn't mean we have to be like them. I have to look at myself in the mirror every day and I'd like to do it with a clear conscience.

It is crucial that a spouse helps maintain a strong sense of values at home by becoming a good example to her children and her husband. She needs to be sensible about her financial choices, allowing the officer to continue his job without the added worry of keeping up with the payments.

I didn't know how to manage money. No one ever taught me how. I was lucky growing up in a family where money was never an issue and when I got married I continued with my old ways. We got more and more in debt and finally everything caught up to us and we couldn't pay the bills. Now I wish I'd been more careful because we've damaged our relationship and I've lost Joe's trust. He's been working extra time to pay off some of the debts.

Retirement

For all the officers and their families who are wrapped up in the struggles of day-to-day living and balancing their financial affairs, don't forget that some consideration should be given to the future years and retirement. You'll be surprised how quickly the children grow up, go to university and then leave you to continue their own lives.

With government cutbacks and offers of lucrative retirement packages to entice early retirement, officers need to financially prepare themselves for the future. Along with the excellent benefits they receive, they also need a financial plan so they can continue enjoying good health and a few luxuries. Start early by talking to a financial advisor who can help you plan for your children's education and your retirement. You won't be sorry!

Along with financial planning, officers and families need to prepare themselves for the psychological effects of retirement. Unlike other professions, policing is a career that 'gets into the bloodstream forever', where the whole outlook on life, the thought process and the ability to act quickly have become a part of the officer's being. Long after the uniform has been put away, the officer still feels the hunger to jump into action when a situation presents itself. Waking up one morning without a badge can cause a sense of worthlessness that can lead to depression. Mental preparation is essential.

Once the officer makes the decision to leave the department he has the freedom to enjoy leisure time. Whether it be a new hobby or becoming more involved in the community, he can finally do what he's always dreamed of. He may decide he would rather continue working but in a different field where he can put those sharp skills he's developed over the years, in a place where they'll be appreciated. Many officers move into other areas of law enforcement, including insurance investigations, frauds, advisory positions or security planning for large companies.

One officer was only home for two weeks before he decided he missed working "Only this time," he said, "I wanted to do something I'd never done before and always dreamed of doing. Car sales," he snickered, "I've always wanted to sell cars. I know a lot about them because I've done a lot of repairs for myself and for other people. I figured I'd done the same job my whole life and really enjoyed it but why not try something different."

Officers can begin to prepare for retirement by first asking themselves if they are ready, then taking the steps to ensure their mental and physical well-being. Some departments offer seminars on dealing with retirement, money management and maximizing tax savings. They will assist them in discovering what is available on the job market and how to develop new skills and write resumes.

Beginning early to prepare for retirement involves taking inventory of yourself, learning ways to look after all your financial needs for future security and taking measures to stay fit and in good health so that you can move into those years with a positive outlook.

I couldn't believe he'd chosen to retire so early; he was only 58 and we still had two kids in university. It just baffled me. George decided to spend a couple of months at home before he started searching for a different kind of job. The first couple of weeks were all right but then he started getting antsy and talking about the guys at work and wondering if the shifts were busy or if they'd done any crazy calls. He was lonely for the job and he was driving me crazy! He talked with a friend who had gone through the same thing only he had waited too long to retire and left with bad feelings about the department. At least George did have some great memories.

After years of sharing the officer with the police department, the spouse can now reap the reward of enjoying the officer's undivided attention. Know that the feelings of loss the officer might encounter, along with any restlessness, anxiety, preoccupation with the job or some depression, are part of a normal process. It may take a couple of months or even a year for him to begin feeling good about himself again, but if there should be other unusual changes he must seek counseling to guide him through a normal but difficult stage of his life.

Most spouses find that the retired officer hinders their daily routine, causing a great amount of frustration and probably a few disagreements. Including him in daily tasks and sharing household responsibilities will lighten the workload and at the same time give him a reason to still feel valued and needed. This will allow you extra time for more pleasurable ways of relaxing.

Set future goals together but take time to grow as individuals as well. This can be a wonderful opportunity to spend time with old friends and to meet new ones.

Retired law enforcement couples fondly recall a past filled with some exciting times and certainly some trying times. They have some exceptional stories to pass along, with many words of wisdom. If you are lucky enough to know or to meet some of these couples, take some time to listen to them. They have endured a great amount of struggling to maintain their family unit and have learned more about the world than most of us have had the opportunity for. They offer some great entertainment and a solid view of what it's all about.

A Heavy Price

The day had begun badly, and by the time Paul reached his last call of the night he was near breaking point. The radio dispatched "child choking." Paul threw on his emergency lights and siren and raced to the small bungalow just minutes away. He entered the house to find the keening mother crouched in the corner of her baby's room with her hands over her face. The helpless father held his tiny limp infant son in his arms. Paul immediately noticed the infant was blue and frothing at the mouth. He checked for a pulse and quickly tried performing resuscitation but there was no sign of life. He continued until the ambulance arrived and rushed the baby to a hospital nearby. Paul knew there was no hope for those desperate parents or their firstborn child.

Paul's drive from the city to our suburban home was long enough to plant the seed of fear. That night he didn't offer me his usual kiss on the forehead, but instead threw his coat to the floor and ran to our six-week-old son Trevor, clutching him to his chest. Without being told, I knew he must have dealt with an extremely difficult call.

For three long nights Paul sat slumped in the white rattan rocker by Trevor's crib, watching his little chest move in and out with each ragged baby breath. There was nothing I could say to reassure him because we both knew that Sudden Infant Death Syndrome could happen to anyone. We became caught up in our own worries and fears and began to experience difficulties in communicating. Our relationship became strained and uncomfortable. It was weeks before we could talk openly about our fears and get back on the road to a healthy relationship.

Knight in Tarnished Armor

Policing is a consuming profession with incredibly high elements of stress. Research suggests that police divorce rates are in the high 70 percentile, which is more than double the national average of ordinary marriages. Three out of every five police marriages end in divorce by the end of the officer's third year with the department.

Spouses experience difficulties adjusting to their lives because of the shift work, the possibility of physical danger and the unpredictability of the job. They find their police spouse's attitude begins to change in the second or third year of his or her career, after continuous exposure to crisis situations. Such traits as cynicism, lack of trust, need for emotional control, perfectionism, jealousy and suspicion begin to develop, all of which are crucial factors in the breakdown of communication. Police officers are accused of being cold-hearted, insensitive and unfeeling, and spouses admit these traits do drift into the relationship.

Spouses begin asking themselves what happened to their perfect marriage and to the excitement of being married to a police officer. The new wife begins her life with her knight in shining armor, proud to be the soulmate for the officer, inviting him to pour out his feelings to her. The spouse coddles him, listens to his countless experiences and works hard at making their home a sanctuary. Soon she begins to find it more difficult to adjust to his career and the changes in his personality. She suffers the backlash of the stress imposed upon her from the job, she feels hurt and frustrated and counts the days when he'll leave the job so that the family can continue a 'normal lifestyle'.

I pushed my way through parents, children and other wives so I

could see David receive his certificate at the graduation cere-
mony. He looked so handsome standing there erect and proud in
full uniform. I just wanted to remember that moment forever, but
it didn't take long to face the uniqueness and challenge of a
police marriage. When I was asked what words of advice I
would give to the new spouse of a law enforcement couple I
would tell them to read whatever they can get their hands on and
to be as humanly patient as they can. Things do get better.

As in any marriage, the partners go through different levels of
changes, but in a police marriage the changes in the officer occur
more quickly and are more intense. It's when the spouse doesn't
change and accept that the couple will begin to experience problems.
Sometimes these problems are difficult to recognize because the couple doesn't realize what is happening at first.

Complexities

Understanding the dynamics and looking for an insider's view on a
police marriage has been a research subject for many psychologists,
writers, police departments and media people, but unless one has actually lived this 'high risk' lifestyle it's difficult to truly understand its
complexities. "This profession has greatly affected my life and the life
of my family," writes the spouse of a New York undercover officer.

An officer facing unrelenting pressures at work and possible
stress-related marital problems at home finds that one affects the
other. Officers are required to perform at top-level capacity at all
times and this can be both physically and mentally draining. The
world becomes a threatening place filled with untrustworthy people,
one that is loaded with dangers, suffering and brutality. He uncon-
sciously brings home all those disillusionments and tragedies, crush-
ing his family's feeling of safety and security.

I was so happy to leave traffic and get back to division. I'd seen too many mangled bodies, children had died in my arms, I've had to locate pieces of bodies on the road and in the ditches from fatal traffic accidents. I mean, how many dead bodies can a person see without it finally taking its toll on you?

There is a heavy price to be paid by the inescapable violence that an officer must face. Their job could entail anything from the grueling task of staying with dead bodies for hours before the coroner arrives, to taking photos of battered wives and children, to trying to comfort a dying person, to following the blood spots on the floor to locate the suspect of a crime. How can an officer be expected to come home in great spirits after dealing with such incidents? Even though the officer suppresses his emotions, sometimes days, months or even years after the incident has occurred, he may suffer the consequences of a particular crisis with flashbacks.

Paul's work with the police department has been diverse. His stories could fill a book but might offend readers with the brutality of the subject matter. Paul has his own way of dealing with oppressive calls, but just recently he admitted that only while watching a coroner's program depicting the many bodies and the circumstances of their death did the full impact of his job really hit him. The faces of hundreds of dead bodies came flooding back, each with its own story, like ghosts that had been released from a locked jail cell in his mind.

Spouses maintain that society's bitter belief that 'cops don't cry' is sadly untrue. Mark remembers:

When I arrived at the home of a young teenage girl who had just graduated from her last year in high school I paused at the steps to collect myself. I had said the same words other times but they always felt so superficial. I wasn't sure how I could change them to make things any easier for the parents. My hands were clam-my when I knocked on the door and I felt that sick feeling in my stomach. I took off my hat and looked at the mother's confused face. I asked if there was anyone else at home with her; that's when reality hits. It's awful. How can you ever get used to doing something like that?

Mark's wife sadly recalled the incident:

Mark sat with the family for hours after his shift, hoping to con-sole them. It had been a fatal accident caused by a hit and run driver. Our daughter was the same age as theirs and it really affected him. When he came home that night, he sat at the kitchen table and cried. I explained to Melissa what had hap-pened and she ran to hug her dad and tell him not to worry about her, that she was really careful on the road. This was a time when Mark really needed us to rally around him, so I can-celed my craft class, Melissa finished off her homework and we rented a movie, made some popcorn and sat around the televi-sion the rest of the evening.

Paul had been called to a shooting at a dessert shop in Toronto. A young woman had been fatally shot during a robbery. Paul talked to her minutes before she died, trying to reassure her that an ambulance was on the way. Weeks later, after the public and the media's curiosity had ceased, Paul continued to feel its repercussions. Each time he drove past the scene his memory recalled the events in panoramic detail.

There is a sense of futility for the officer in being unable to change what he sees, and he might be dealing with these situations without any outlet to vent that stress. This can cause the officer to be debili-tated by a disorder known as 'post-traumatic stress'. "Police suffer three times the amount of stress as civilians," states Dr. David Purvis, a British psychologist and psychotherapist who has studied trauma and its aftermath. "Between 7 and 15 percent of any police force suffers from stress problems at any given time."

Officers who have been involved in shootings or violent cases can become anxious, suffering intense emotional stress, eating and sleeping disorders and marital problems. The situations that might trigger post-traumatic stress are not always critical ones. They may be from the strain of many events over time. Even though an officer may try to ignore the fact that there is a problem, it is up to the intuitive spouse to spot the changes and be there for him as a sounding board, perhaps providing some gentle prodding and solid support. An article in the Ottawa *Citizen*, dated February 24, 1998, is entitled "Trauma: Second-guessing a split-second decision."

"In the aftermath of a police shooting, the surge of adrenaline that first rushed through the brain starts zooming through the rest of the body, sometimes causing a range of physical problems, from impaired hearing and vision to a sense of the world moving in slow motion," says Staff Sgt. Robertson. "Officers sometimes have trouble sleeping or experience flashbacks."

Says Sgt. Gravel: "Within 48 hours or so, I started to lose simple little things like just automatic motor skills. I couldn't fall asleep because I would stop breathing. If you tried to eat, you'd just throw up. You'd be so proud of what you'd done one minute, because you knew that you did the right thing based on your training. And you'd be so devastated in the next minute, because you actually took somebody's life and you couldn't believe that you'd done that. And you really wondered, 'do I really want to do this for a living?'"

Once the situation really sinks in, the officer can start worrying about how they're going to be judged for making that split-second life-or-death decision and second-guessing their actions.

On his first night back to work about a week after killing Mr. Jackson, Sgt. Gravel was dispatched to a warehouse, where an alarm was sounding. "I go to the back of the warehouse and the back door is open. It's still a hot summer night, I'm standing there on the (train) tracks and the track cracked all of a sudden. I hit the ground thinking that it was a shot. My shirt was soaking wet with perspiration."

"In the worst cases," says Staff Sgt. Robertson, "the initial trauma can turn into a long-term mental paralysis, in some cases post-traumatic stress disorder, leading to major depression, personality change and an inability to cope with the world."

One patrol officer from Toronto Police confirmed the detrimental effect that stress can have on one's physical health.

The jolts got so bad that I would wake my wife up through the night. I'd buck, arching my body backwards and then forward as if an electrical current was raging through me. Sometimes it would even wake me up. I finally saw a doctor, who said it was the stress I was suffering while waiting for blood tests to return after being bitten by an Aids victim on a call.

Officers need to know that reactions to these situations are normal and should never be looked at as a sign of weakness or as destroying their 'macho image'. Stress reactions are usually only temporary and denying the problem can be crippling to the officer's job and his marriage.

Each officer has his own way of dealing with stress, but should take any available courses on stress management that are offered through police departments. If they recognize that they are having a problem they must make the effort to visit their Employee Assistance people, who can provide the guidance the member will need to get through a few tough weeks, and can put him in touch with people who have been through the same experience.

Stress in the Family

Spouses can be affected by the same stress their police spouse suffers. Law enforcement couples have learned that if the officer is unhappy the family is unhappy. Many spouses who responded to the survey acknowledged that they at times felt the symptoms long before the officer recognized them.

She was always bitchy. It didn't matter what shift she was on or off, she was always on my case. I knew the guys at the station had been giving her a really hard time because of her recent promotion and she had just been involved in a case of a double teen suicide, and the grueling images began giving her nightmares. I became so caught up in her life and her stresses that I found I couldn't function properly at work just worrying about her. I would come home after work and have a few drinks so I could deal with my feelings. When I tried talking to her, she said it was me that had the problem, not her. We ended up going to counseling together, but only because my mother intervened and brought us to our senses.

Couples receive little training on how to meet the challenges of stress. Families, friends and peers of police officers are often the first to see a change in attitude. If you are aware of a police couple having difficulties and recognize they need guidance, use a tactful and loving approach to let them know. Some law enforcement families are so caught up in the emotional and psychological complexities that they may not be aware of where the problems started and it may be too late to repair the damage. Don't be sorry and wish you'd said something earlier. Do it now!

One wife recalls sitting in the kitchen listening to the constant tap, tap, tapping of her husband's foot against the leg of the table at each meal.

He would hit the table with the side of his foot and beat out a tune along with the accompaniment of a utensil. It just about drove us all batty. He didn't even know he was doing it until we threatened we'd eat in the other room. He would stop for a little while, then he'd be back at full force. One night the kids and I brought some instruments of our own to the table, a nut cracker, some chopsticks and a grater. We figured if we couldn't beat him, we'd join him. Little did I know the kind of stress he'd been under. When we played our little rendition of 'Ants go marching' he threw his spoon across the table, hitting one of the kids on the arm, mumbled something about 'what did we care' and left the house. When he came home much later in the evening and the kids had settled down and gone to sleep, he explained that he had been conducting an interdepartmental investigation of an officer he knew and the events were really upsetting him.

Some officers who are working on more classified duties may choose to protect their family by remaining silent, avoiding any hen-pecking they might receive at home. They feel their home is a place in which they are not criticized. This kind of pent-up silence causes failure in communication.

I can't understand how come I can deal with all kinds of crisis situations at work, but when I get home I can't make any peace in my own marriage.

From the beginning of his career, an officer is trained to control his emotions on the job. There are numerous times when he wishes he could throttle someone who really deserves it, but he learns to restrain himself. After years of controlling feelings of sadness, anger and revulsion, he begins to become uncomfortable in showing intimacy, passion, warmth and caring to his wife and his family. This is the beginning of the 'blue wall' set up to protect himself from showing any emotions.

I'm 23 and I still wish I could hug my dad but that was a no-no when I was growing up. He used to pat our heads. He wasn't demonstrative that way and I think it was because he was a cop. It's kind of hard to start now and I find I have a hard time showing my feelings to him.

Eventually the officer finds he deals with his home life in much the same way he deals with his work. The spouse waits for the officer to come home so that she can discuss the day's activities, only to find the conversation is one-sided and he's in a bad mood.

I had a domestic where a distraught wife called for police protection. Her husband was beating her with a coal iron. When I arrived to rescue the wife and handcuff the drunken husband, the wife turned on me. She kicked me in the groin and called me a 'f' pig and told me to get the _____ out of her house. I was frustrated beyond belief but maintained my cool, that is until I got home. I walked in the door to see my two-year-old pulling the dog's ears and in retaliation the dog greeted me by peeing on the carpet. I lost it. I gave him a swift kick down the stairs, spanked my two-year-old, and like a lunatic ran ranting and raving at my wife for her lack of parental guidance and laziness. I'd upset the whole family and it had nothing to do with them. It happened all within 60 seconds of being home. I had to learn how to deal with my anger before I got home.

The immense emotional control these officers develop can produce an aggression that results in physical or verbal explosions. A spouse can console an officer who is hurt or upset but may have difficulty dealing with one who is angry. Spouses must learn to distance themselves from an argument until the police officer is calmer or it could become a battle that leads to more serious consequences.

The public may also perceive the officer during the course of his duties as uncaring and cold; they are unable to understand it is simply a defense mechanism. But the mask he wears at work becomes harmful to his relationship if he can't peel it off when he gets home. He may begin to feel he has no one to confide in except other officers. Spouses who have tried probing for information find the officer distances himself even further, developing a code of silence that excludes his family from a very large and important part of his life. This barrier forces the family to feel like an outsider. As one officer described it, "Policing is like a double-edged sword...we keep the moral fabric of society together but have trouble keeping our own."

One Royal Canadian Mounted Police wife explained how they handled this obstacle.

He used to come home after a difficult day, defeated. He didn't want to talk at all. I tried to get him to open up but he acted like a robot. That made me really mad and I'd end up starting an argument. I'd tell him he was an unfeeling jerk and he'd tell me I was a hysterical nag. When the argument got heated he'd suddenly turn off and become frighteningly calm and silent. Very alien from the man I married. That's when I'd really get nervous. We were drifting further and further apart and I finally decided to call a few friends whose husbands were police officers and feel the situation out. I was surprised to find that they had the same kinds of problems. They helped me deal with a lot of my fears and anxieties. Now when he comes home I tell him about my day, trivial things that he doesn't have to think about. If I have a problem I want to talk about, I wait until he's been home a couple of hours and he's more relaxed. I give him the space he needs. Most times now I find it only takes a little while for him to settle down and then he's happy to share the day's events.

Many spouses complain that they feel the officer is unable to emotionally connect with them and has difficulty in showing affection. The officers are nervous about letting down their mask in case their vulnerabilities show. They become less demonstrative and more like the 'cop at work'. This is another side of that emotional control trait. In the survey spouses admitted that open communication was at times difficult and other times strained. One spouse when asked if her husband's job had any emotional effect on her replied:

Oh, yeah, right now I feel a great amount of envy. I wish I were the cop and he was the wife.

The spouse must discuss her frustrations with friends, family or a counselor, and in this way provide an outlet for any suppressed feelings. Developing some hard and fast rules about communication right from the beginning can provide the basis for a stronger marriage.

He includes me in everything and he tells me a lot. I got so caught up in his police work that my job paled in comparison. Nothing seemed as exciting. We share both the difficult experiences he faces and the very few joys. This gives me an advantage in understanding him and he gets the privilege of a sounding board and an unbiased point of view.

Another spouse married for 10 years says it has been a lot of really hard work.

If I had to choose, I'd marry my wife all over again. Our rela-
tionship has never been boring. With her mood swings and the
constant challenges I face in my own line of work we have lots
to talk about. The only problem is finding the time to do it. We
never seem to both be in the same mode of relaxation at the same
time. It can be a real struggle. We have to consciously make an
effort to listen to each other and spend times together when
we're not so tired. When we're together we have a lot of fun.

Officers who are having difficulties in their relationships find that
the emotional control at work becomes weakened. Letting down their
emotional guard at work can be dangerous. Sven, a patrol officer with
the department for 16 years, remembers a very difficult time in his
marriage.

We just got to the stage where we seemed to be fighting all the
time. It was the same thing—she'd say it was me and I'd say it
was her and we'd call each other some pretty bad names, really
hitting below the belt. I still loved her but I didn't know what the
problem was, and it was on my mind constantly. One shift I
walked through a small city park and noticed the pigeons
scratching for food. It brought back a memory of a park we used
to visit when we were first married and where she used to scatter
a little bag of bread crumbs for the birds. The memory really hurt
and I got teary-eyed. I was so wrapped up in my sorrows I didn't
see a truck that had just robbed the bank, coming straight for me.

Spouses eventually understand that the destructive traits that officers display at home are actually their talents at work. Their discretion in decision making, in forming immediate judgments with very
little information, are used in every aspect of their work, from decid-
ing whether a child should be taken from its family to determining

who caused an accident or a quarrel, or where a weapon is hidden. Decision making in the home is usually left to the spouse because of the role she plays in the marriage. There is a conflict when the wife has had the control and has been making the decisions and then the officer arrives home ready to take control of a situation, sometimes acting before he knows all of the circumstances.

Cop at Work, Cop at Home

He may be unable to make the change from being the authoritative figure at work. This is when parenting becomes more difficult and battles ensue. The officer who is used to looking at a situation at work as 'good or bad', 'breaking the law or not', decides what kind of action needs to be taken without realizing he's doing the same thing at home. Once again he wins the unpopularity contest.

I always felt as if I were being reprimanded or he was going to give me a ticket. I felt talked down to, as if I were the criminal on the street. I thought it was weird the first couple of years we were married, but I've just tried to accept it. I'll worry about it when he starts shining a light in my face.

Michelle would not clean the basement. I argued with her for 15 minutes and she persisted with the excuse that homework was more important. Paul walked into the family room, reprimanded me for being too soft with the kids over the years and allowing the kids to become lazy and ungrateful. He demanded Michelle clean the basement immediately. The two of us (Michelle and I) suddenly became the enemy and we defended each other. Paul succeeded in getting her to do the job, but what he didn't realize was that he had hurt both our feelings. The people he deals with on the street are not the people he has to live with at home.

Suspicion

After continually seeing the darker side of humanity, and being constantly lied to, the officer develops an underlying attitude of distrust and a suspicious nature.

Trevor and his friend Brian were in their early teens when they felt the first real sting of Paul's suspicious instinct. One warm summer evening the boys disappeared without telling us where they were going. Paul became immediately suspicious and thought we should take a little run to the more familiar teen gathering spots. We checked the convenience store, the malls and the park close by, with no sign of the boys. But he was not about to give up. Driving up a neighboring road he detected the boys sauntering along. Paul's hawk eyes immediately noticed something flickering in Trevor's hand.

"Hang on, we're pulling a U-Turn," he said in an exasperated tone. "I think Trevor's got a cigarette in his hand."

Paul pulled up to the side of the curb, jumped out of the seat and grabbed Trevor's arm, pulling a lighter out of his hand.

"What's this?" he demanded.

"Just a lighter, Dad," Trevor responded. Brian immediately dropped back into the shadows.

"What are you doing with a lighter?" he questioned.

"Just foolin' around," Trevor said, looking to his friend for support.

"Let's just see what's in your pockets, boys," he demanded.

I yelled at Paul to get the kids in the car and go home and talk about it there, but he was like a dog with a bone. Trevor and Brian pulled out a few items and handed them to Paul, who walked to the car headlights to inspect them. A group of adults had collected at the corner from their night walk and stood curiously watching the scene. I felt sorry for the boys; they were being interrogated as if they were criminals. Paul asked them a few trick questions, trying to trip them up. He accused them of smoking something. Trevor was devastated.

How could his Dad not believe him, and how could he embarrass him in front of all those people and his friend? Paul went as far as going to the convenience store to speak to the owner and ask if the boys had been there to buy cigarettes. The boys had no traces of anything else on them, nor did we smell smoke.

This was a patterned response from Paul's constant interrogations in cases at work.

Like most concerned parents, Paul and I both worry the kids might become involved in drugs. Paul is far more protective because of the hundreds of kids he's seen whose lives have been destroyed by drugs. Paul is acutely aware of any changes in the kids' personalities, their body language and behavior. Suspicion does become a part of every police officer's disposition, but explaining to your family the reasons he reacts to situations in this manner can help to alleviate some serious damage in relationships at home. Some spouses have found they too begin developing that overprotective and suspicious nature because of the constant subjection from their husband.

Dave was on night shift when a friend called asking if I would like to go to the movies and out for a drink. It was a Friday night and I'd had a rough week at work and thought it would be a great way to relax. We had dinner, saw a movie and then sat at a donut shop and talked for a couple of hours. Dave had tried calling home a few times and left messages. "Hi, guess you've gone out, call you later," then "Hi, still not home, O.K., call later," and finally, "Where the hell are you, you've been gone for six hours!" After listening to the messages I knew exactly what was going through his head. He was suspicious that I might be having an affair. He coughed when he came into the bedroom in hopes I'd be awake. "Hey," he said "What's up?" I was tired and didn't feel like being his suspect and made to feel guilty because I'd gone out with a friend. I didn't feel like explaining but he had to be satisfied. He asked a whole string of questions until finally I got mad. We ended up fighting and I threatened to call my friend so she could verify where I was. I guess what makes him a good officer was making one really trying husband. It wasn't worth the effort; it was better just to hug him and tell him where I'd been without getting my back up.

For an officer, suspicion is a crucial element of protecting himself at work. He has been trained to faultlessly observe and listen to everything around him. He's been directed to watch a person's every move, to identify what they're wearing, be suspect of what they're doing, notice how they speak, and look for small quirks that might distinguish them immediately from someone else. He looks for any possible motivations that person might have for being where they are or doing what they're doing. He constantly evaluates people for possible threats. This can cause an officer to seem paranoid or distrustful to his family and friends.

I remember going to a friend's corn roast party and a bunch of us joined the farmer for a wagon ride through the fields at night. One police officer was visibly uncomfortable. He sat stiffly with his back against the boards of the truck while the rest of us wrestled each other for straw stuffing. He mentioned we should sit still or someone might get hurt and to be aware of what was around us. "You never know what's out there," he said. "There might be someone with a gun." At the time I thought it was a really odd thing for someone to say, but since then I have become involved with a police officer and it doesn't seem so strange any more.

Officers find they prefer to sit with their backs to the wall where they can examine what's going on around them. One officer's wife said it was a real pet peeve with her. She would purposely run for the 'power seat' at a restaurant before her husband got to it. She would watch his uncomfortable response at being put in a position where he felt he lacked cover and protection. She thought it might force him to pay more attention to what she was saying but instead he didn't listen at all; he was too busy looking over his shoulder at what moved behind him. They drove each other crazy until finally she let him claim his seat back.

One spouse refused to go shopping with her husband.

It was a really trying experience; instead of shopping he was always watching the people move about and looking at their parcels. His suspicion finally rubbed off on me. I was at the department store doing some shopping when I noticed an older man walking up and down the isles. Most people would probably think he was just a normal shopper, but after years of Bob pointing out people's mannerisms and peculiarities I noticed this guy kept looking around the store and picking up items but not looking at them. I decided I should report him to security just in case and it turned out my suspicions were right on. He had stolen a number of expensive items. The store thanked me with a gift certificate and I got some really good mileage out of the story.

Cynicism

An officer will undoubtedly get to the cynical stage of his career. This occurs because of their distrust in human nature. They begin to view the world as a negative and unsafe place for themselves and their families. They develop the 'us-versus-them' attitude, where they feel everyone is out to get them, and they begin withdrawing from society and sometimes their own friends and family. The only people they can trust and that understand them are other police officers. Once they have lost regard for the law and society they become resentful, and again the vicious cycle begins. They know they can't take action so they hold it inside and become the victims of cynicism. Cynicism is one of the main corruptions of the police profession and a major destructive force in a marriage. Spouses claim it is cynicism that causes the officer to become 'changed' as a result of police work.

One of the ways an officer counteracts cynicism is by developing what's known as 'black humor', a distorted, bizarre view of the oppressive part of society and of the terrible things they see. It's a professional toughness that enables them to survive what they encounter on the streets.

An officer was called to the Toronto subway for a 'jumper'. He arrived with his pen in one hand and a half-eaten sandwich in the other. The body had been decapitated and he had to search for the missing part. He walked the rails, eating his baloney sandwich, until he found what he was looking for. He asked the stricken subway driver to 'catch'. The driver subsequently ran to the closest garbage bin to be sick. No one would find that remotely funny, except a cop or perhaps another emergency response member.

Cynicism can also cause an officer to become stressed and finally lead to a burnout. Those beginning their profession are anxious to save the world, only to be rudely awakened after a few short weeks on the road. Studies have proven that there is an increase of cynicism during the first 10 years of service and then it begins to level off. They deal with so many negative issues that they begin wondering if there is any good left, and then ultimately believe there is none.

It didn't matter who we talked to, Jack was always sure the person wanted something from him. We were at a dinner party and one of the guests was telling us about his daughter getting a ticket. Jack immediately thought the guy had an ulterior motive—

you could just tell by the way he straightened his back and his eyes formed into little slits as he peered at the guest. He always thinks the worst of everyone. I have to really watch myself because he makes us look at people with the same mentality.

Overprotectiveness

Overprotectiveness is another common problem seen in law enforcement couples. The police officer's perception of what an undesirable person is can have an impact on his family. He becomes more critical of the choice of friends his spouse and children make and it only takes a quick calculation for him to determine their place in his home. If he doesn't approve, he lets his family know it. He's doing his best to protect them from being hurt; what he doesn't realize is that this can cause a great deal of resentment even if he's right—and he usually is!

I didn't like the guy as soon as I saw him. There was something about the way he wouldn't look me in the eyes when I talked to him, the way his head hung when he shuffled by us. I told Breen, our 18-year-old, that he didn't seem seriously interested in her and that he looked shifty. Of course that's the wrong thing to say to your daughter, just makes her more determined to prove I'm wrong. This guy eventually showed his true colors, by standing her up at the semi-formal. He told her it was because he'd "lost track of time." Breen pretended it didn't bother her but I think she knew I was right.

Jealousy

There is no worse killer in a relationship than jealousy. Some spouses become jealous if the police officer is partnered with another of the opposite sex. With the many changes to the police department over the years females now have the opportunity of working in a field that once was male-dominated. The fact that they work in close quarters for 10- and 12-hour shifts can make any spouse become immediately possessive and cause her imagination to go wild. That jealousy is not only targeted at policewomen, but at the amount of time the spouse feels the officer spends with his colleagues after work. This becomes a problem if she feels he should be spending all of his time off at home.

I couldn't stand that he was working with a female cop. She was single, tiny and new on the job. John always enjoyed being with the new recruits, but this one wore perfume. I sat at home day after day and night after night worrying he would have an affair. It didn't help that they worked late sometimes. I visualized them sitting in the car rubbing elbows, sharing food and conversation in the close quarters of the police car. I knew she'd laugh with John because he had such a great sense of humor. When he arrived home after a shift I'd sometimes get a faint whiff of her perfume and I'd go crazy. Even though John assured me that he was not in the least bit interested, I found myself checking his pockets, calling his cell phone while he was working with what I hoped were bits of interesting information about my day that might interrupt any possible intimacy between them. It didn't help that most of the guys on his shift were unmarried or divorced. It was really hard on our relationship. I found I was always questioning him, looking for any signs that he was being unfaithful. He finally told me I needed help and offered to speak to a sergeant about being partnered with someone else. If he brought home flowers I thought it was to hide his guilt. I started eating to dull the state of helplessness I felt. I thought I must seem boring to him after coming home from his exciting job and some young chick. The wake-up call came via my sister-in-law, who told me that if I didn't open my eyes I'd lose John. He was really hurt that I mistrusted him. It almost destroyed my marriage.

One police spouse said she feared the police groupies most.

There's a group of women out there who have this thing about uniforms and the symbol of authority that they represent. They don't care if he's married or not; he looks like a challenge. That makes me really nervous.

There is a definite masculine influence that officers have on some women. Whether it is the combination of the uniform, their size and build, and the fact that they look so good, or whether it's because they might be a challenge and they are untouchable, something makes them appealing. And the temptation is there for an officer just as it is in any profession.

Gossip about officers having affairs is strictly that…gossip! If a partner decides he is not happy in his relationship he may become unfaithful, regardless of his occupation. If there is no trust, there is no solid background for a marriage. You must be determined to work hard at any relationship for it to be a successful one.

Spouses have had other concerns about the officer working with a female. There is a fear that she may not have the physical strength to protect her partner and might be too emotional to handle a crisis situation. This is untrue and a needless worry. Police officers have all been trained to protect each other in any manner that is necessary. Don't forget that female intuition has been known to be felt long before a man's.

Living in a Fish Bowl

Choice of friends has often been a one-way street for law enforcement couples. Officers' narrow 'us-versus-them' view of society, along with the belief they are living a fishbowl existence, scrutinized by the public, their neighbors and even their friends, forces them to seek friendships with other police officers.

Jackson couldn't even sit on the porch with a beer without someone looking over. They were nosy, wanted to catch Jackson at something he shouldn't be doing. Jackson finally got fed up and sat in the backyard where he had a little more privacy. Of course, sometimes that kind of shallow attitude depends on the area one lives and the kind of neighbors one has.

Socializing with other police families is easier because they share the same lifestyle and similar experiences. Spouses found that because of the constant broken dates with non-police families due to shift work and overtime, even the closest of friends would give up. One police spouse admits that many friends have drifted away and she can understand their frustrations.

They had invited us to dinner three times and I had to cancel all three because Dave was called in or had to work late. They just finally gave up and I couldn't blame them.

Many spouses in the survey wrote that they had few non-police friends and found that the isolation was stressful. I don't remember why I took the position I did when Paul first started the police department. It was partly because I had maintained a close bond with my childhood friends and perhaps partly on a strong intuition, but when he accepted the job I had only two requests. That he call if he was going to be late and that we did not strictly socialize with other police officers, but also enjoyed the friendships we had nurtured over the years. It took a lot of rescheduling and it was a struggle at times, but we always found time, even if it was just a couple of hours, to enjoy their company.

At one time in Paul's career we disliked going to parties or social functions. As soon as people found out Paul was a cop he became the center of attraction. He was surrounded by people who threw questions at him about the different aspects of the law and about news involving crimes and policies, and asked questions about getting tickets fixed and where radar traps were set. Then there were the ones who were eager to slander officers by reiterating tales about cops abusing their power or others on the take. We used to try changing the subject but it inevitably came back to the same topic.

Other spouses found that they would enter a party environment and the room became hushed. People worried that the officer would be watchful and critical of how much they were drinking or how they were acting. Some may have felt guilty about something they'd done in the past that wasn't legal.

Because policing is a consuming profession, an officer must learn to relax and remember how to be a civilian. Police spouses agreed that maintaining friendships with non-police friends brought a 'normal' perspective of life back into focus. It allowed the police officer to see that there are people out there who respect our laws and what they stand for.

Police families have encountered situations where their home becomes a police station for neighboring people who need advice.

It's when they start calling at home and you have no idea who the person is. He identifies himself as your mother's neighbor's friend George, and then he goes on to say that he hopes he's not bothering you but could he speak to your husband about a ticket he got on the highway to Alaska!

Living in the area in which the officer works can pose other difficulties. Neighbors and friends may feel uncomfortable calling the station with a problem if they know the officer on duty. Some law enforcement families found that their homes became the local hangout or the mini police station. The fishbowl existence, especially for officers in small towns, can be extremely stressful for the family.

If a neighbor spotted a suspicious person, or was in trouble or got a ticket, they called our house looking for Joe. It got so that we never had any privacy. I took in stray dogs and cats for people who didn't know what to do with them, housed runaways and neglected children. We have four teenaged boys so it seemed at least one of their friends was always getting into trouble. At one point I thought I was going to have a nervous breakdown. Joe was never home and when he was, the guys from work always turned up at our door. It got pretty crazy sometimes.

Attitude and Burnout

The authority and responsibility that comes with the job, along with carrying a gun, is a pretty intoxicating experience. Most officers know this feeling is normal and that it only lasts a short while. There are, however, some who never recover. These officers are few and are not liked or respected by their peers, and their warped attitude destroys their relationships at home. Usually these officers find that police work is not the right career choice for them.

Attitudinal and behavioral problems are the first signs of burnout and stress. Officers begin to show signs of problems in their intimate relationships at home. Those who believe burnout will never happen to them may be faced with symptoms that could very seriously affect their health and their judgment. In a crisis situation at work the result could be injury or even death.

Separation and Divorce

We have discussed the many factors that play a part in the high divorce rate within the police department. It is easy to find countless officers who are on their second or even third marriages. They agree that the demands placed on them by their job affect their home life.

Eighty-two percent of the spouses who answered the survey or were interviewed felt that their police partner let the commitment to their career take precedence over the commitment to their relationship. New law enforcement spouses find they are unwilling or unable to adapt to the demands of the police career. Some give up early in the relationship, while others continue to struggle, never understanding where the problems lie and how to get over the barriers.

Not me. I'm staying married; besides, I am too damn stubborn to give up. I put too much into this relationship to see it all go down the drain.

We'd been married for seventeen years and I'd had enough. I was worn out raising three kids, trying to keep everything and everyone together, rearranging schedules, meeting everyone's demands but my own! No one seemed to understand how I felt, not even my mother. Alex and I discussed ways to resolve the problem but I guess too many years had gone by, too many fears, too many changes. Poor Alex was always good about bringing flowers and being attentive; the problem was he never seemed to be around. I saw a family counselor and finally decided I should leave and go out on my own. I couldn't expect him to give up his job at this point and I just didn't want to be in the same rut. It was a sad time for about a year but Alex continued to visit me and helped to look after some of my financial needs. I began dating but found I was only comfortable around police officers. I

*learned a lot about myself that year. Actually, we're back togeth-
er again, and things are working out fine. I guess I changed too.*

Separation and divorce places an enormous burden on the family.
Recognizing and then admitting there is a problem, communicating
with each other and seeking a solution are crucial in saving a marriage. Sometimes, though, couples must accept that the marriage is
not repairable. When too much damage has been done and all
avenues have been exhausted, they may need to go their own way.

Alcoholism

Some ways of coping with stress can be destructive. The frequency
of alcohol abuse within the police department is known to be consid-
erably higher than in the general public. Drinking might start as an
innocent social release, a time to unwind with other officers. Those
officers who do not share their work frustrations with their spouse, in
order to protect them, choose instead to share them with their fellow
officers who will be more understanding. For them, drinking is a
masculine approach to dealing with a problem without seeming like
a 'wussy' or a 'wimp'. It starts with a beer after work, but then it
becomes a regular routine, and can continue at home. It can endan-
ger his career and lose him the trust of his family.

*I knew I needed help when my suitcases were out on the steps
after getting home from having a few drinks with the guys. The
note attached to the case read: 'You need to dry out. Do yourself
a favor and get help.' At first I was really mad and was ready to
kick the door down, but then it came to me like a pail of cold
water in the face that I was about to lose everything that mat-
tered. I'd made a big mistake. I drove to my mother's 400 miles
away and stayed for a few days, then started going to A.A.*

In an article entitled "The Demons at the Bottom of the Bottle," one officer remembers some pretty desperate times:

Then again, in any policeman's drunken haze the job has a hand if you look deep enough. It's there somewhere, lurking. I certainly remember blaming the job as I looked down into the four fingers of smoky smelling liquid I'd come to rely on.

I remember my final lucid day before the drinking started, before I faced losing my job. It was the day I split up with my wife and moved back with my parents....I was lonely and had a desperate feeling of failure.

Speak to someone? No way. Policemen didn't talk about their problems. Your colleagues discussed your problems among themselves in the canteen while you were out on patrol.

That Monday I began night duty. I had a few pints before I turned in for work. As I didn't drive to work or drive police cars, with a drunk's misplaced confidence I reckoned I was in the clear. I took in a bottle of mouthwash and arrived on time. As I got changed a friend told me he could smell the drink. I told him I wasn't surprised because I'd been pissed for two days. He thought it was hilarious.

Spouses of officers are not immune to becoming dependent on alcohol. Those who are unhappy with their lifestyle, who are unable to adjust and are lonely and depressed, drown themselves in the bottle.

I started by treating myself to a couple of glasses of wine at night just to relax before going to bed. We were going through a pretty tough time. He was gone a lot and I had just lost my job and wasn't getting much support; the kids were young and demanded a lot of my time. When our savings account was spent, I became depressed and started to drink more, and Mike would go

*out and have a few drinks with the guys, which made me feel
lonelier, and it became a vicious circle. After a few months I
found I couldn't get through lunch without a glass of wine, and
a few ryes after dinner. I didn't go out anywhere, yelled at the
kids a lot and gained 20 pounds. We saw a counselor for a year
after I fell down the stairs in a drunken stupor and my brother
found me lying in my own vomit.*

Alcohol abuse is evident in every lifestyle, but again, the added
stress in police work makes it more prevalent. Besides early recognition of a possible problem, the department can offer other ways to
help officers unwind and relax. Some offer full exercising facilities,
sports programs, hobby and school courses. A healthy way to relieve
stress is by naturally feeding the mind and body.

Suicide

When an officer feels trapped with no escape and no release he may
feel his last resort is suicide.

"Suicide Stuns Force" appeared on the front page of the Ottawa
Citizen on May 10, 1995. Below the headline Leonard Stern writes:

Young officer faced inquiry in drowning. Const. Shawn Wilson
had been one of the officers under investigation after a man flee-
ing police drowned in the Rideau River in March.

At least a half-dozen marked and unmarked police vehicles
crowded the street outside Wilson's home shortly after his wife
found his body around noon. Wilson had shot himself with a rifle.

Police suicides are the highest of all stress-related jobs. The par-
ticulars leading to suicide are more complicated due to the types of
stress they endure on the job. There are a number of indicators of a

suicidal person such as stress, burnout, Traumatic Stress Syndrome, marriage problems, lack of communication, financial problems and feelings of being rejected and isolated. The future outlook may seem bleak and they become desperate to diminish the pain. Alcohol can be a large factor in suicide attempts, and the availability and familiarity of guns make suicide easier.

Help!

If you notice any of the above symptoms, find help immediately! Pick up the phone and call your doctor, hospital emergency or even the police station. Do not wait! It could be a matter of life or death!

Researchers have concluded that people suffering from extreme stress and burnout can bring destruction to their relationships and their jobs, and can cause their immune systems to break down. An officer needs to recognize that his job greatly affects his family, who can also develop the same kinds of stress symptoms.

The department has become more active in their role of support toward officers and their families, providing some programs, classes and counseling. They recognize that families can adapt and adjust for a short time but that eventually their resources will be depleted. The main problem occurs when officers will not admit their depression and will not ask for help. They've been heard to say, "Save it for the guy who really needs it."

Providing a mandatory program, with coping strategies that will benefit both spouses, should be a prerequisite for all departments. This program would assist in education and at the same time help prevent further problems. The program should start in recruit college and continue through to retirement, and would help officers and their spouses to understand the demands of the career on the family at different stages of their lives, and the effects it has on all members of the family.

The department must provide a 'professional' program, with

trained leaders, designed to support spouses throughout the officer's career. Spouses would then come to see the programs as an avenue of learning and release rather than a 'coffee clique'.

Making the Marriage Last

Many of the problems that have been identified in these chapters have already been recognized by the law enforcement couples. Some have yet to experience any of them.

We undoubtedly share the common denominator of this 'high-divorce lifestyle' and the serious occupational demands that police work has on the family. To avoid crisis we must continually educate ourselves, being realistic about the stresses we will face and developing the strength and fortitude to overcome them. Working for a 50-50 partnership is difficult in any marriage but it is especially trying in a police marriage. Look for support from family, friends and outside sources. Working actively toward a happy and secure family can provide the officer with a positive contrast to the negative aspects of his work so that he can contine to do a good job.

Staff Sergeant Cassidy from 32 Division, who has been with the Toronto Police Service for 28 years, states:

The success of any relationship must be a mutual decision. The definition of a successful marriage is: the mutual progressive realization of a worthwhile dream or goal.

In speaking to police spouses at different stages in their marriage and of the officer's career, I found they were thankful to be given an opportunity to have their say, but at the same time they were cautious in protecting their spouses' identities. Some were happy to reveal their names, many preferred to remain anonymous, but all of them were pleased to give their advice in the hope it would help new law enforcement couples.

Gloria Boothby, the wife of Chief Dave Boothby of the Toronto Police Service, who has been married for over 35 happy years, attributes their success to a number of things.

We received a great amount of support from family and friends. They always let us know that they cared and we knew we could depend on them.

Develop a strong sense of independence. Don't rely on your partner to keep you happy. You need to find that fulfillment on your own and to develop a life of your own. I took university courses to upgrade my knowledge and look after my future. You never know when you'll have to manage alone.

It is important to plan goals together. Having a common destination or dream enables you to work together, share an interest and look forward to the future.

I would recommend mandatory spousal programs, and spouses should make an effort to attend. It will give them a better understanding of what's involved and how to value the relationship for the positive aspects of the job.

On Mary's wall next to her husband's shift work schedule she has pinned a reminder:

Love knows no limit to its endurance,
no end to its trust,
no fading of its hope;
it can outlast anything,
It...still stands when all else has fallen.

1 Corinthians 13:7-8
Phillips Translation

Carol Soave, who has been married for 26 years to Ben Soave, inspector in charge of the Toronto Integrated Intelligence Unit for the Royal Canadian Mounted Police, lives a most interesting lifestyle. Owing to the type of work involved in the Intelligence Unit, their family has been posted in countries all over the world, allowing them the privilege of some wonderful experiences, along with a few frightening ones. Carol spoke wistfully for the better part of the evening, relaying unusual occurrences and exhibiting a knowledge of people and their countries that most of us would never have the opportunity to experience. Her insight into keeping a marriage together comes from the experience of a very trying lifestyle.

We probably stay together because Ben's gone up to 40 weeks a year. Seriously though, you get used to it. When he comes home we settle any business matters and discuss what's been happening in each other's absence. It was understood from the beginning that I ran the household while he was away. We had a mutual understanding of defined territories. He was not allowed to interfere with my decisions at home or to cross that line because I had to develop a routine for myself and the kids.

You have to be really supportive of his career. I knew that he couldn't be really good at what he was doing if he was always getting flack at home. When he's away, I lead my own separate life and he leads his, but when he comes home I drop everything and cater to him. I believe in 'till death do us part', so putting aside my individual life is easy. I do things solely with him. Friends and family understand our routine.

Carol tells young spouses:

You start out with such high expectations when he first begins his new career—maybe he'll be the chief...but five years down the road you find he's not the same person you married. He becomes more secretive and withdrawn. You may not necessarily even like him any more. This is a crucial time when you must make the ultimate decision to accept this kind of lifestyle or not. If you do then bite your tongue, and if you don't, then get out early because he'll be unchangeable. We all change, but officers change a lot more.

Theresa Bartley has been married for 24 years to Frank, a police constable with Toronto Police Service, and feels strongly about her commitment.

Having faith in God is really important. If you have faith you don't find you're blaming other people or things for your problems and you have less fear that something might happen to him on the job too.

We talk about things and deal with our problems. It's the one thing we always believed was really important and it's worked for us.

Frank was happy to give his input as well.

What makes our marriage a good one is faith, encouragement for each other, love, patience, understanding, commitment and desire. We always focus on our marriage because the couple comes first.

Cathe Carnell, married for 23 years to Sergeant David Carnell of York Regional Police, is resolute about her advice.

The best advice I can offer to the spouse of a new law enforcement couple is that the 'team' must be prepared to accept that the job comes first. It's the nature of the beast. Officers have no option but to be at the mercy of the police department, the public and the courts. When an officer first applies for the job, the couple rarely stops to think about the consequences. They see a profession that comes with a guaranteed position, good starting salary and great benefits that are very attractive. It feels like a safe haven of security but, in reality, the job is in a system that is insecure and unforgiving. If you want a strong family unit, an officer's spouse should not hold a demanding career, if the marriage is to be 100 percent successful in traditional terms, unless the relationship involves two police officers or they are extremely exceptional people. The spouse needs to be able to pick up the slack and sometimes the pieces when her husband's working.

Cathe believes her marriage has survived despite her lack of coping skills when she and Dave first married because she quickly learned to become independent and able to compromise.

Becoming independent is at the top of the list. You have to be able to take control of the emergencies in your life and make quick decisions without counting on your spouse. Not because they don't want to be involved, but because they sometimes just can't. We have to be the captain of the ship and our husbands are second mates at home, when they are home! Financially they keep the ship afloat, but we make the ultimate decisions. We learn to be strong and to compromise, not just for our husband but for the job.

When your husband comes home angry, you must learn to recognize where that anger comes from. Usually it's because he's frustrated with work and what he experienced that day. It is a love-hate relationship for him. He can't snap at the public no matter how stupid the situation, he can't sound off at the brass or the judge, so he brings it home. A spouse shouldn't retaliate; it only causes more problems. Some spouses pass it off without worrying about it and others try to talk about it. No matter how you handle it, be prepared to carry some of their baggage and anger because they can't possibly cope with getting rid of all of it. You must be an extension of him because he sees so much of the darker side of society and, unlike us, is not privy to some of the wonders of life. You'll find that when you start to understand him he will become your best friend.

Cathe's husband Dave feels strongly about the reasons their marriage has been successful.

If you're going to be successful in this profession, you have to share with a spouse like Cathe, a person who is prepared to be a part of the good, the bad and sometimes the really ugly. It is impossible to keep it to yourself, and if you don't have that kind of person to turn to, then you should consider a new life or the job will eat you alive. There is nothing 'macho' about it.

I respect those who have put the badge down to save their marriage. They probably didn't realize it at the time, but they were saving much more than just a relationship. Life is no dress rehearsal; you only do it once. No matter how noble you think policing and serving the community is, sometimes the personal and family cost is just too high.

To everyone you are just a number and a badge. When you are abused on the street, have your life threatened and are then criticized after the fact, only your spouse and family will be there to truly understand. Sure, you have the camaraderie of your colleagues and the backing of your association, but they don't go home with you and they're not there in those times you need someone most.

Dave tells all officers who have succeeded in their career:

Hey, my hat's off to them. I congratulate them and their 'very significant other'. Don't forget that success is because 'behind every good cop, there is an even better spouse'.

Helen Chambers, who has been married for 45 years to Bill, who has retired from Toronto Police after 35 years of service, recalls:

You learn to have a lot of patience and trust. Bill used to go on stake-outs and was in plain clothes and he would always send a message somehow to say he was okay. I had to trust that he was at work. In the '50s, rules were different. I remember a police officer who was married and had an affair with a clerk and they were both fired. I think there are more temptations, with no restrictions out there now. We would never go to a party without our husband, but now young wives wouldn't think twice. Maybe the spouse has become too independent.

A spouse whose husband is a sergeant with the Royal Canadian Mounted Police and is posted in different areas feels success is what you make it.

If you marry an R.C.M.P. officer he has to become your best friend and your primary family. Because of all the moves, other family connections get strained. You can't always get to visit your parents for holidays; therefore, your home has to be the focus of your life—not your house, because that changes so often—but the atmosphere created in the house, which moves with you.

The wife of a Toronto Police officer answered the survey with these words:

After reading through and answering your survey I realize just how much I do at home to keep my marriage and family a close-knit unit. One thing I work toward is always including my spouse in what goes on while he's working. That way he always feels part of the family even when he's at work. Often he feels left out when he misses an event with one of our children, so we adjust to include him by calling him or saving things to show him, trying to give him lots of notice regarding important dates so he can arrange for time off if necessary. We also wait for meals so he can be included whenever possible. Regarding his participation, it is one area where the kids and I always compromise, plan and include him.

We are very close. There is no ego competition between us. Actually, my spouse has lost sleep, changed shifts just to accommodate us when necessary, and we've done the same.

Susan Tucker believes that a sense of humor is essential in the success of a marriage.

My husband was the R.C.M.P. member on duty the day I had a minor traffic accident coming out of our driveway in Alberton, P.E.I. Because I was at fault, he had no choice but to issue his own wife a traffic ticket. That evening, my mother phoned to say she was going to put his birthday gift on the bus. When I told her about the ticket she became flustered and said she probably shouldn't send the gift after all as he might be offended. I told her not to be silly, that we would appreciate it, whatever it was. I was curious to know why she was so upset. The next day we had a great laugh when we discovered his birthday gift was a

"Precious Moments" figurine of a policeman issuing a traffic ticket. The figurine was entitled "It Is Better to Give than to Receive."

For Better or for Worse

When he first put on the uniform
I was so proud, but things unknown
since then, so many thoughts have changed,
so many times our plans rearranged.
The countless hours I sit and stare,
and silently I shed a tear,
as I watch the families all togther
I know that things will not get better.
The thankless job of theirs alone,
the hours spent away from home,
for the man who wears the uniform.
The hours pass into the years,
the feelings change, greater are the fears.
The man I love, the man who is there,
for many people to cheer or leer,
I stand by him, but things unknown
I still am proud, but stand alone.

P.C.'s wife, 14 Division
Toronto Police Service

As I note in the Introduction (and feel it bears repeating here), the problems that face law enforcement couples are numerous. Some are lucky enough to have encountered only a few of the obstacles discussed in this book, and others are just beginning to notice changes in their relationship, but many will be desperately struggling to piece together the puzzle of this distinctive lifestyle. There is no telling when the changes will begin but they *will* begin. Pulling yourself out from under the blanket of pity and working to keep your relationship healthy should be your number one priority and must be established right from the start.

There are going to be times when you feel like giving up, when you're bone tired of rearranging your life around police schedules, tired of being disappointed, tired of the fears, the changes and the hard work it takes to keep your relationship happy and successful.

You are already aware that the officer needs a balance of work, family life, home and hobbies to help alleviate stress, but what about your stress? Does anyone care that you are not recognized for the amount of stress you endure?

Working at any relationship is difficult at best, but a police lifestyle is definitely a challenging one. Be assured that it can also be a rewarding and exciting relationship if you first accept that the officer works an emotional job with extremely high demands and that he must make an immense commitment to the job. You can then be more sympathetic to his case, and when times get tough you'll find that you need not search too deeply to admit that you are very proud of what he does and that you truly do love him.

There have been millions of books written about love and what love is all about, but in the case of a police relationship love must be very much a 'team effort'. When asked what kind of advice she would give a new officer's spouse, one woman, tongue in cheek, replied, "It's too late for advice." Another spouse suggested:

Know what you're getting into first. His job is going to be a really big part of your life, so try to experience the shift work before you get married, and talk to other police wives.

Advice was given in great abundance, with love and empathy for new spouses. Communication was the number one recommendation, followed by building a strong support system, becoming independent and acquiring a good sense of humor.

If I had to do it again, I wouldn't change a thing. I couldn't possibly live without the excitement and insanity of a police life. Anything else would pale in comparison.

It is the inability to adapt to the demands of the job that causes marital problems in law enforcement couples. Do not let these demands poison a healthy relationship.

1. Learn good communication skills. Talk to each other about the day's events and any problems that might arise. Share your future goals. Talk, talk and talk, but then know when *not* to talk. Don't forget to listen. Anyone can listen, but it takes skill to really understand what's being said and to be able to read between the lines.

   If I notice Bob looks edgy and he's scowling, I don't force him to talk about his day. I usually find he needs time to relax and then he may or may not want to tell me what's upset him. He usually does come around, though. You get to know when you should be open for them and when to wait a while.

2. Be aware. Keep an open mind. Your partnership cannot always be 50-50; in fact, you may feel that you are carrying the heavier load, but be relieved to know this is normal in a police relationship. Things do ease up, especially when kids get older. You will eventually find you have more than enough time for each other. *It's only temporary.*

3. Be understanding and patient. Try to understand how the offi-
    cer's job affects him.

    A wise young police spouse said:

    *If he's had a difficult day I just let him blow off steam. He
    rants and raves and carries on until he's spent, then he feels a
    lot better and we can get on with our night.*

    Another spouse, whose husband has been with Toronto Police
    for 20 years, says:

    *He developed such a change in his attitude and his personality
    that I felt I didn't know him any more. When he gets funny like
    that I try to keep my cool, calmly let him know it's time to come
    back to earth. He always tells me I'm his 'pillar of strength'.*

4. Be flexible. Like a tree that is rooted but whose branches sway
    back and forth, you must give your family stability and at the
    same time be able to yield to the changes you'll encounter.

5. Be independent. Develop yourself as an individual apart from
    'the cop's wife' and you will achieve a stronger sense of self.
    This will enable you to have the fortitude to endure some criti-
    cal times and disappointments.

6. Learn to forgive. When times get tough sometimes people say
    things they don't mean.

    Try not to forget there will be days the officer sees and experi-
    ences some pretty terrible things, which most people would
    never encounter their entire lives. Forgiveness does *not* mean

you'll lose your pride. Forgiving is a much greater step toward becoming a better person and at the same time maintaining a strong relationship.

I handed out three tickets for speeding and every one of the drivers fed me a lie. One man said he had a bee in his car and was afraid it would sting him so he sped up in hopes it would fly out the window. He badgered me and nattered at me, insisting it was not his fault. The next guy told me he had a malfunction with his speedometer and that his mechanic couldn't find the problem so he had to drive with a broken speedometer and that's why he was speeding. The last person argued that he was late picking his mother up from the hospital where she was undergoing treatment. He tried starting a fight and I ended up arresting him and taking him to the station. At first the stories are entertaining but after a while the lies become so blatant they make you angry. I got home late and noticed that every light in the house was on and asked my wife if we were supporting hydro on our own this month. She gave me some weak excuse and I just blew. I took three tickets' worth of anger out on her and she certainly didn't deserve it. I'm glad she understands me and can be so forgiving.

7. Develop a sense of humor. It is the most effective way to avoid problems and arguments. Humor can change the 'emotional climate' and allow you to face up to your responsibility in an argument. Laughing is proven to heal the heart and get you through some pretty trying times.

Try to understand the police officer's sense of humor. It may often sound dry or callous but it is their way of releasing tension. Believe it or not, at some point in your marriage you will suddenly find yourself not only understanding it but appreciating it as well.

8. Learn to trust. Trust your partner. If you begin planting seeds of doubt in his mind you will destroy the intimacy and closeness you've always enjoyed. Know that he loves you even when it's difficult sometimes for him to show emotion.

    Despite rumors you may hear about officers having affairs, be assured that most often it's just idle gossip. An officer generally is not interested in having an affair with anyone, and especially not with an officer of the opposite sex, if he's content at home. He would never risk jeopardizing his family.

    One spouse, who is on her second police marriage and is committed to making this one work, said:

    I get angry 'cause he's never home. How do I know he's really in court, or working overtime? You can't get him at the station. At first I just wanted to get back at him so that when he was home I'd make plans to go out and he'd see what that felt like, but he starting losing trust in me and I almost destroyed our relationship. Now, rather than get suspicious and angry, I try explaining my feelings. I let him know when his work is too demanding and that not being able to spend time with him makes me unhappy. I told him that sometimes a 30-second phone call can make a big difference.

9. Work at it. No relationship is easy. Hard work and perseverance will help make a marriage successful. Develop a positive attitude and promise yourself that you will work at making your marriage last because you value the relationship. Be committed.

Be a friend and give unselfishly of yourself. Be willing to make sacrifices to keep your relationship healthy.

I remember thinking that every cop was destined to get divorced. Only one guy on my shift was still married, two were single, and the rest were on their second and third marriages. My new wife and I attended a police wedding and I wondered how long this one would last. Some of the guys placed bets on a five-year max. What I didn't know was that my wife was fearing the same thing. We both agreed that it really doesn't matter who you're married to, it only matters that you really work at it.

10. Everyone loves to be loved. There is nothing that makes living more worthwhile than love. Give it freely and unconditionally and it will always come back tenfold. Be demonstrative in your affection to your spouse. Touching, kissing and hugging let your partner know you love him.

11. Give praise. Tell each other that you are doing a good job. Everyone needs a little pat on the back sometimes to make them feel worthwhile; it nurtures the ego and the spirit.

12. Don't nag. It's hard, but don't complain. The officer has enough people doing that at work that he doesn't need to hear it at home as well. He likes to know he can enjoy quiet and peaceful surroundings. One officer was proud to announce:

I know that I have support and love always waiting for me at home, and that's what keeps me doing a good job at work.

13. Be there for him. When your spouse needs to talk or just wants your company, be available for him. After all, if the kids demand

your attention you give it to them; if your friends need you, you try to help; so if the person who has the toughest job of all needs you most, then you should be there for him.

What I love most about coming home after a really crazy shift are the little things that Anna does. In the winter she might have a fire going, or has a little note posted on the message board or a card from one of the kids that says, 'I love you, Dad'. She makes coming home so great that I can put the job aside and enjoy my own little nest, where everything seems like a fairy tale in comparison to what I see from day to day.

14. Keep balance. Because of the multitude of lifestyles the officer experiences, his home should be the place where life is put back into perspective. His family provides a contrast and a sense of balance, harmony and routine.

15. Make time to be together. This can never be stressed enough. Make dates and get away for a weekend or even just for a coffee. It's a wonderful way to keep that loving bond intact.

16. Be positive. Having to put up with negative people and situations at work, the officer does not want to deal with them at home as well. An upbeat and positive attitude is like a good sense of humor; it can overcome any problem.

When I complain to her about the social problems of our society, the prejudices and the issues, she always points out positive reasons why it's great just to be alive. I don't know what I'd do without her enthusiasm and great attitude toward life.

17. Stay interested. Show an interest in his work and hobbies. Even

if they don't make you rapturous, spend some time listening and asking questions. You might be surprised at what you learn.

18. Educate yourself. Learn everything you can about the officer's job so that you can cope with any problems that arise. Read articles, books and magazines about police officers and their families. Inform yourself about what the department offers in the way of spousal programs and benefits. This will allow you the comfort of feeling secure.

19. Socialize. Go out and have some fun. Divide your time between non-police friends and police friends. One offers support and a common denominator, and the other offers a more objective point of view and a sense of normality.

20. Watch for the signs. Stress is the largest factor in law enforcement family breakdowns. A crisis can be avoided simply by recognizing that the officer is having difficulty managing. Listen to the cries for help. Look for the early warning signals such as changes in behavior, crankiness, forgetfulness, sleep disturbances, mood swings, weight loss, poor eating habits, feelings of anxiety, or anti-socialism. Also keep an eye out if he develops a temper and quarrels easily or seems continually depressed. If it is left to get out of hand, coping with a large amount of stress can result in divorce, alcohol or drug abuse and sometimes suicide.

21. GET HELP!! If you or your spouse are suffering from any or all of these stress symptoms, please, please don't wait—get help! What you are going through is not a sign of weakness. Find a friend, a family member, clergy, doctor, counselor, or call your Employee Assistance people, and be assured that they will lead you in the right direction and at the same time maintain your confidentiality.

Don had witnessed the brutal abuse of a baby who suffered in the hospital for days before she finally died of a brain hemorrhage. Both parents were arrested and both had no remorse for what they'd done. Don went to the hospital every day until that baby died. It took two months before I started to notice changes in him. He sat around and watched television all the time, didn't want to go anywhere, developed large black stains under his eyes from lack of sleep, and he wouldn't talk much. One day I noticed some bruises on the inside of his arm and I started to panic. Of course I thought the worst. When I asked him about them he admitted he pinched his arm really hard to get the image of the baby out of his mind. That's when we both realized he needed immediate help.

22. Experience a ride-along. The best way to understand what the officer's duties consist of and what he must contend with is by joining another officer on a busy night shift. You'll have a totally different outlook. The experience will be worth it!

23. Become involved. By taking time to become personally involved in your community you will not only help others but will continue to project a positive police image. Lobbying for a good cause such as Mothers Against Drunk Drivers, helping victims and their families, or lobbying for tougher laws can also help ensure an easier future for the officer. You might think about becoming more involved in the changes occurring within the police department that will affect the officer's career and your life.

When my wife is on night shift I always play around on the computer and I have learned a lot. I know that older people are intimidated by computers, so I thought I would volunteer my knowledge at senior citizen homes to teach them how sim-

205

*ple and fun a computer can be. It's great to see the eyes light
up when they learn to play a simple game.*

24. Join a police spousal group. Phone your police department to
    inquire about their spousal group. If they don't have one, call
    your closest department and ask if you can hitch on with them.
    Sitting at home worrying or griping about how tough you have
    it is positive energy wasted. Listening to other spouses and shar-
    ing your experiences and difficulties can be enriching. It's been
    proven that the attendance for these programs is poor. It is real-
    ly important that you make the effort. If nothing else it's one step
    further toward a better marriage.

25. Start your own group. If the department does not offer a group
    for spouses, then start one in your area. Begin by calling the peo-
    ple you know and sending the message by word of mouth, or try
    placing a short ad in the newspaper or police magazine. You
    might be pleasantly surprised. Sharing the joys and hardships
    and establishing a good line of communication with other spous-
    es will help nourish good relationships and form a strong bond
    of understanding. Invite non-police friends and family to help
    cultivate a sense of normality and to teach them how to support
    a law enforcement couple.

26. Try personal coaching by telephone, over the Internet or by per-
    sonal appointment. Oftentimes spouses would prefer not to dis-
    close their problems to a group. You do not need to be a
    licenced counselor. If there are problems which require profes-
    sional assistance, recommend the Employee Assistance
    Program or a professional who can help. Try to work with your
    Employee Assistance people; they can share numerous pieces
    of information.

27. Teach friends and family. Don't be afraid to let friends, neighbors and family know about your lifestyle and its difficulties. Tell them you need their support. Give them literature to read or spend a little time discussing the different aspects of police work.

28. Pray. Prayer is a wonderful way to put everything in perspective. Developing physically, intellectually and spiritually, separately and together as a family, will allow you to feel whole and complete.

At one of our favorite cafes, my dear friend Donna eagerly handed me a rolled-up piece of paper secured with an elastic. It was at a time when we were all going through our own little crises and I remember feeling a great weight lifted from my shoulders. It read:

Good Morning! This is God.
I will be handling all of your problems today.
I will not need your help.
So relax, and have a great day!

Appendix A

Codes of Ethics

Law Enforcement Code of Ethics

As a Law Enforcement Officer my fundamental duty is to serve mankind; to safeguard lives and property; to protect the innocent against deception, the weak against oppression or intimidation, and the peaceful against violence or disorder; and to respect the Constitutional rights of all men to liberty, equality and justice.

I will keep my private life unsullied as an example to all; maintain courageous calm in the face of danger, scorn or ridicule; develop self-restraint, and be constantly mindful of the welfare of others. Honest in thought and deed in both my personal and official life, I will be exemplary in obeying the laws of the land and the regulations of my department. Whatever I see or hear of a confidential nature or that is confided to me in my official capacity will be kept ever secret unless revelation is necessary in the performance of my duty.

I will never act officiously or permit personal feelings, prejudices, animosities or friendships to influence my decisions. With no compromise for crime and with relentless prosecution of criminals, I will enforce the law courteously and appropriately without fear or favor, malice or ill will, never employing unnecessary force or violence and never accepting gratuities.

I recognize the badge of my office as a symbol of public faith, and I accept it as a public trust to be held so long as I am true to the ethics of the police service. I will constantly strive to achieve these objectives and ideals, dedicating myself before God to my chosen profession...law enforcement.

Family Law Enforcement Code of Ethics

The Law Enforcement Code of Ethics is instilled into each officer during training and at graduation, and is taken very seriously. Each graduate knows that the job can be difficult but equally rewarding. An officer's future with the police services is unlike other professions, the officer must learn to deal with innumerable situations involving all the complexities of life and human nature, both negative and positive. Because of the nature of this job, the officer's family must be aware of the hardships involved and they too must take their role as family members and supporters very seriously, enforcing strong values in their family unit and setting an example to society. The Family Law Enforcement Code of Ethics is a guide to ensure stronger family ties.

As the family of an officer, part of our fundamental duty is to work together to help safeguard the family's well-being so that the officer may return home and recover his sense of perspective. We will do this by providing a loving and relaxed environment so that he feels welcome and appreciated. We will make an effort to communicate so that we may understand each other's hardships and work together to solve them.

We will recognize that this lifestyle is "different" and accept it as a positive challenge, being constantly mindful of each other's welfare. We will see each other without judgment and become our own very best self so that we may create a strong relationship with unquestioned trust and understanding. We will strive to find some sense of order in the disorder, self-appreciation in times of loneliness, creativity in chaos, and time to be together when there's never any time.

We will not insult the officer's choice of profession by selfishly demonstrating our personal feelings toward something he can't change. We will understand that he takes his commitment to the job very seriously. Officers are constantly under pressure to uphold their private lives as an example to others and as a family we will also strive to uphold those beliefs.

We recognize that living with a police officer can be extremely trying but we will wear our invisible badge with commitment and pride, and ride the wave of excitement and realism with him throughout his career. We will always strive to achieve these objectives and ideals, dedicating ourselves before God to help the officer do his very best in his chosen profession...law enforcement.

Affix the Family Law Enforcement Code of Ethics to your refrigerator as a reminder that when this lifestyle becomes too difficult you can be reassured that you are not alone. Ask yourself what really matters and see the picture as a whole.

Appendix B

Surviving Shift Work

But I have promises to keep,
And miles to go before I sleep.

Robert Frost

For the Officer:
Good Night, Sleep Tight

An officer must be sensitive to his body's needs and must learn to recognize that sleep is imperative to his health. With the change of the day/night cycle an officer tries to adjust himself to the unnatural signals. A fatigued officer cannot function properly at work or at home. Here are some easy ways to help ensure a better sleep.

1. Continue your regular bedtime routine, relax before bed with a good book or soft music, take a warm bath, dress for bed, brush your teeth and get into bed underneath the covers.

2. Caffeine and liquor are stimulants. Do not drink for at least four hours before bedtime.

3. Reduce your liquid intake to a minimum so that you are not awakened through the night by the call of nature.

4. In the middle of a bright summer day, lawnmowers, kids screaming and dogs barking never allow for a restful sleep. Close windows and keep out the sun's rays with black-out linings affixed to the back of curtains or shades. Keep the room cool with an air conditioner or a fan. The drone of a fan can

aid in blocking both indoor and outdoor noises.

5. Remind your family and friends that you are asleep by hanging a sign outside your bedroom door and the front and back entrances.

6. Your biological rhythms have difficulty in adapting to day/night and dark/light. You may find that you can't experience a deep restful sleep. Try acquiring at least seven hours of sleep, even if you find only four or five of those hours are a deep sleep and the remainder of time you are resting. If sleep is difficult to attain, try the old 'counting sheep' trick or go through a simple routine of stretching each limb and then relaxing—whatever works for you.

7. You must learn to safeguard your sleep. Be tough about the sanctity of getting enough. Impress upon family and friends how important your sleep is to survive.

8. Female officers have more difficulty adjusting to shift work. They feel it's solely their responsibility to carry the entire load of domestic work and raising children. Learn to delegate household duties. Be aware that shift work can cause severe mood swings and affect hormone production. Talk to your physician if you experience difficulty when on certain shifts.

9. Your family needs their sleep too. When you arrive home after a night shift, have the same respect for them that *you* would expect.

10. Learn to identify your mood swings during a change of shift. Determine how many hours' sleep you need to feel good. Identify the times that are most difficult and be courteous enough to tell your family, "I'm sorry, I'm just really tired. Give me a couple of hours to wake up and I should be okay," or "I'm really sorry, midnights really drag me out and make me moody. Please be patient." You'll be surprised at how quickly family members will understand and be willing to

accept your crankiness if you're honest with them.

11. Speak to your physician, local health unit or association for information on shift work.

Shift-Lag

The body's circadian cycle continues to operate in a "normal" fashion during shift work, thus leaving the officer with the sensation of jet lag. Trying to remain awake during the course of a night shift and during the drive home can be a serious problem, with very serious consequences.

1. It's more difficult to focus on paperwork at 3:00 a.m. Instead of struggling through it when you're least alert, try getting it done at the beginning of the shift.

2. If you get the 'nodding head', call a fellow officer to meet at a coffee shop where there is more light and action.

3. Leave your window wide open to circulate fresh air.

4. Protein foods produce amino acids which enable the brain to become more active. Enjoy foods such as a bagel with light cream cheese or crackers with light peanut butter, or pack a lunch including beans, lean meat, poultry, fish or eggs. Snack on carrots and celery sticks, popcorn or pretzels; their crunchy sounds will help keep you awake.

5. Exercise great caution driving home. There are enough hazards in your job without further endangering your life with dangerous driving. If you feel tired, take a power nap at work before setting out for home. If you begin to get tired halfway home, open the window and turn your radio to a station that has a catchy beat, and find that singing voice you never thought you had.

6. Be honest with yourself. Admit when you are too tired and pull over to a safe spot. Leave your emergency lights on and

take a deep stretch or a vigorous walk around the car. Challenge yourself with some invigorating exercises that will increase your blood flow and get your heart rate up. If this doesn't help, lock the door and take a power nap.

Eating for the 'Health of It'

Along with the irregular hours of shift work come irregular eating habits. A diet lacking in nutrition can greatly effect an officer's health and productivity. The irregularity of police calls has the officer scrambling for fast foods, which are washed down with cold coffee or warm pop. Make it a habit to prepare your own foods, keep a healthy schedule and you will find that you feel great and sleep more soundly.

1. Keep your regular eating habits of three meals a day as if you were on a daytime schedule.

2. Be selective about what you eat. Lunch less often at fast food restaurants that prepare foods high in fat, salt and sugar. Pack your own healthy lunch, following your food guide and using a little imagination. If you eat out, don't be afraid to ask the cook to prepare a low-fat meal.

3. Use herbs to flavor foods rather than butter, sour cream or sauces. Learn to bake or broil foods rather than frying them. Nothing tastes better than chicken on the barbecue with a side order of mixed vegetables lightly brushed with olive oil. If you want dessert, try fruit dipped in yogurt, gelatin or angel food cake topped with berries.

4. If you like to snack, be aware that chocolate bars and chips trick you into feeling more energetic. They only pick you up for a short period of time. Instead, try foods high in complex carbohydrates such as popcorn, pretzels, bagels, rice or pasta. These foods can also help you in relieving stress.

5. Eat a small healthy snack before going to bed to avoid acid

build-up and eat a good breakfast when you get up. This will fuel you throughout your busy day.

6. Police officers are known to suffer from digestive problems such as heartburn, ulcers and hiatus hernias. Avoid these problems by eating foods rich in fibre such as fruits, vegetables and whole grains. As much as possible, avoid alcohol, coffee, and spicy or fried foods.

7. When you're off shift, try your hand as head chef. Learn to shop for nutritious foods by reading the labels. Visit your library or local bookstore and find cookbooks that boast hearty foods that are helathy and fun to prepare. Good choices are *Lighthearted Everyday Cooking* by Anne Lindsay or any book put out by heart, diabetic or dietetic associations. Or ask a friend to recommend their favourite. In the summertime prepare meals on the barbecue, and in the winter experiment with easy soups and stews that will be welcomed by everyone.

8. When supper is over and everyone has complimented you on your great culinary skills, get everyone to pitch in with the clean-ups so that you can spend quality time together.

9. There is some debate on the use of vitamins. If you are undecided, speak to your family physician.

10. No matter what shift you're on, make time to join your family for a meal, whether it's when you get home from midnights and you join them for breakfast, or when you get up and enjoy breakfast while they are having dinner. This is a great time to discuss the day's (or night's) events. It's being with them that counts!

Fit for Shift

Keeping fit is one way to minimize the negative effects of shift work. In the survey conducted, 70 percent of police spouses admitted the officers were overweight due to a fast food diet and lack of exercise. Look after your body and it will improve the quality of your life.

1. Everyone knows that smoking is dangerous to your health, so why not begin by quitting?

2. Alcohol not only puts on weight but causes a number of diseases, including high blood pressure. Drink in moderation.

3. Take the time to set yourself a fitness program or ask a trainer to help you. Many clubs offer the services of their employees to evaluate and help you through a program of your own. Take advantage of it.

4. Work yourself into the program slowly, with a stretching routine at the beginning and end of the workout. This will keep your muscles from being injured and increases flexibility.

5. Use the fitness room in your station. Start work a little earlier, work out during your lunch hour or stay after work. If your station does not provide a fitness room, initiate a plan whereby interested officers raise money toward a fitness room of their own. Your example could start a healthy trend.

6. If you can't find time at work then set aside half an hour to an hour at home and take a brisk walk through the neighborhood or do your own workout in front of the television with a good exercise video. If you can afford equipment, try a treadmill or rowing machine. Just keep moving!

7. Nothing can be more fun then enjoying a game of baseball or soccer with your family. You get the benefit of exercise and the added enjoyment of being together.

8. Exercise is proven to act as a sedative. It will allow you to relax and get a better night's sleep as long as it's done three hours or more before bedtime.

9. There are many ways that exercise will help enrich the quality of your life—it improves digestion, enhances your immune

system, tones and firms up your muscles, improves circulation and helps reduce blood pressure, reduces tension and relieves stress, builds strength and improves endurance, increases your metabolic rate, enhances coordination and balance, strengthens your bones, enhances oxygen transport throughout the body, improves liver function, strengthens the heart, improves blood flow, increases weight and heart size thereby deterring heart disease, decreases cholesterol and triglycerides, improves breathing efficiency and can also decrease your appetite after working out, not to mention improving how you feel about yourself.

10. Be disciplined. Once you begin, exercising becomes addictive. You'll never be sorry!

11. Remember that a fit cop is a safe cop.

Daily Communication

Living in the crazy schedule of a police lifestyle, communication can become difficult, with the result that you may lose touch with your loved ones. Communication is the single most important means to a better relationship with your family.

1. Absolutely always find time to discuss problems that occur at work or at home. Family members cannot guess what's going on in your mind. Talk about it and they will be most willing to lend a helping hand or a kind word.

2. Find the time to be intimate with your spouse. Find a sitter and take a weekend away together. Children need a break from you as well.

3. Take an active part in your children's life. They are only young once. They deserve as much of your attention and love as you can give. Give quality time.

4. Make that added effort to talk to your teenagers; they can too

easily slip into a world of their own and become less approachable. Join them in one of their favorite television programs and listen when they talk—their small talk can be 'big' talk.

5.	Always keep your family up-to-date on your shift hours, court time, overtime and paid duties. There is a small sense of security in not having to 'wonder' where you are and it will allow them to make plans of their own.

6.	Leave special notes on a blackboard or dry erase board. Tell them you love them in person and in writing.

7.	Invest in a cell phone. Hearing your child say "Ma Ma" or "Da Da" for the first time can be the most wonderful experience even if you can't *see* them.

8.	Many officers 'hang out' with their buddies who share the same time off. This kind of socializing can lead to 'the party life'. Get together occasionally to share a few stories but remember your family needs your friendship too. Find a hobby or interest and pursue it.

9.	Help with household duties when you are off shift. This will relieve some of the burden your spouse may be feeling after one of your long shifts. Give her a break so that she will feel more relaxed and can better enjoy your company.

10.	Help make your absence on holidays and special occasions easier for your family by enjoying the little time you do have together. A little of you can go a long way. Think of little ways to give of yourself, especially when you are on a shift—a quick phone call, a note left on her pillow or some flowers delivered to her door.

For the Spouse:
Love You, Love You More!

Shift work is one aspect of police work where the officer's family is constantly being challenged and where you must learn the virtues of patience, kindness and love. Creativity is definitely an asset when applying for this job. The pay is low but you'll find in the learning process that the rewards are extremely high.

Keeping the home a quiet haven so that the officer can sleep can be enough to cause even the most composed person to feel unnerved. Social schedules, eating schedules, sleeping schedules can be a nightmare for the most organized person. Using common sense and strict organization are important, but it is crucial to be available to listen, understand and give your undivided attention, support and love.

1. Don't allow this lifestyle to become a burden. Look at it as a challenge instead, one that can make or break your family. By enforcing family commitment you will teach children the most important value of all.

2. Try to keep the 'noisy' chores for later. Instead, use this time of shift to do quiet menial chores, work on a project, a craft or school work, or go for a long walk. Don't cook or bake; aromas from the kitchen can interfere with your spouse's sleep. Do not use shopping as an excuse to leave the house when he's sleeping. This could end up destroying your budget and his trust. Instead, visit with a friend or family member.

3   Changing your schedule to revolve around your spouse can be difficult and frustrating. This is not a good lifestyle if you are the least bit selfish, but making changes will bring you closer together.

4. Let friends and family members know when your spouse will be sleeping, either verbally or by providing them with a calendar of his schedule.

5. Develop a plan for little children while your spouse is asleep. Enjoy the mornings with plenty of physical exercise, an exciting experience at the library or programs that are provided by your municipality. In the afternoon you can share quiet times

working on activities such as crafts, reading or watching a movie.

6. Organize a group of police spouses in your neighborhood and alternate visits depending on the spouse's shifts. This will also allow you to share your problems and solutions about your unique lifestyle.

7. Keep a sign on the door announcing that your spouse is asleep. Keep one on the back door so that teenagers and their friends are also reminded.

8. Teach your children at a young age that sleep is very important for the officer. As they become older, you'll find your constant nagging will have paid off.

9. Unless there is an *emergency*, do not wake the officer. Take what you need from the room *before* he falls asleep.

10. Be more conscious of how you decorate the sleeping area. Keep the colors warm and inviting, completely cover the windows and use materials that will darken the room.

11. Try to achieve some kind of regular pattern in this erratic and irregular lifestyle. It takes discipline, creativity, planning and implementing. You can do it!

12. If your spouse had a choice, he would pick a regular lifestyle rather then shift work. When he feels tired and irritable and occasionally takes it out on you, remember to be patient and understanding and gently remind him he's not acting his normal self. Remember what it felt like after two or three nights of cramming for exams, or when you were up all night with infants for weeks on end. Remember he probably feels that way a lot of the time.

13. Spouses of officers often find themselves alone and performing many roles in the rearing of children. When you feel as if you've been saddled with all the responsibility, it's time to take a break. Find a reliable babysitter and call a friend to join

you in an evening of fun or relaxation. Taking time away from home and the kids is healthy for everyone.

14. Even if you feel you are the main disciplinarian, stand behind your spouse when he is off shift and disciplines the kids.

15. Spouses usually find they are the ones who schedule family meetings and get-togethers. This becomes more difficult with teenagers who have busy schedules. Once you've decided that you are going to have a family night (against all their protests and wild excuses) stick to it; it will pay off in the long run.

16. There is nowhere in the world your spouse would rather be during a holiday than with his family. It's up to you to create memorable times by digging deep into your imagination. These will be the memories that will bond you with your children forever.

17. Don't feel sorry for yourself because you don't feel you're living a 'normal' lifestyle. Begin your own family traditions and you'll find that being a little bit out of sync with the rest of society can have many positive results.

18. Officers often feel detached from their families when they work a seven-day shift with court and overtime. Send him off with little homemade gifts from the kids and a love note or two from you. Everyone likes to feel needed and appreciated.

19. Keeping in touch verbally during those overwhelmingly long shifts is important. Invest in a beeper or a cell phone. This will eliminate any fears you may have in case of an emergency and it will allow the officer to still feel a part of the family when he hears baby talk, listens to the children saying their prayers, tells his teenager a funny story that happened at work or gets to say "I love you." It's worth every cent!

20. Mealtime and preparation can be chaotic in a police family but by following some practical suggestions you will find it becomes easier. The name of the game is to keep a routine but

still be flexible. It's difficult getting everyone together for a meal even at the best of times. If you set dinner for 5:30 p.m., ask everyone to be there at 5:00 p.m. This allows plenty of time to delegate duties such as preparation and table setting. Be flexible enough to change that time to 4:00 if your spouse has to leave for work early. The most important goal is to get everyone together at that table.

21. In this society working families need meals that are fast and nutritious. Luckily we now have grocery stores that understand these needs. Purchase foods with healthy ingredients. Make use of crock pots, one-pot dinners, casseroles, stir-fries and quick pasta meals. When you prepare one casserole, it's just as easy to do two or three and then freeze for another meal.

22. Spend one morning or a day to prepare meals for the freezer and to wash and prepare vegetables and fruit. It will save you time and puzzling over what to make the rest of the week.

23. Who says pancakes are only for breakfast! Sometimes breakfast and lunch meals are a treat for dinner. They are quick to prepare and enjoyed by the officer who doesn't like a heavy meal when he wakes up after sleeping all day.

24. The microwave is a must in a police family. Cook a full meal (a turkey, chicken, meat loaf or roast beef in large portions) to be sliced for sandwiches or cut up and frozen for quick dinners by just adding a few of your favorite vegetables.

25. Delegate, delegate…don't feel the responsibility is always yours. Teach the kids and your spouse to cook. Take turns shopping, preparing meals and cleaning up. It will serve them well some day.

26. Invest in a few healthy cookbooks that provide recipes for quick and nutritious meals.

27. Teach your family to eat healthy. Leave a food guide on the

refrigerator door and don't buy snacks, junk food and pre-pared foods; they are expensive and unhealthy.

28. Loneliness due to shift work can be debilitating unless you learn to like yourself and your own company. Try to find hobbies and interests that will keep you occupied when your spouse is at work. Learn to relax and enjoy your time alone. Most people dream of being in your shoes. Believe me when I say that if you can make it through the first couple of years, you'll look forward to evenings and midnights when you have the whole night to yourself. Because we have such busy schedules we forget what to do when we're bored. This is a good time to pamper yourself.

29. Develop compassion. Put yourself in your spouse's shoes so that you can understand how he feels. This way you won't feel sorry for yourself. Focus on the bigger picture. The sooner you realize that you can't change your lifestyle the quicker you'll develop a wonderful lifestyle of your own.

30. Make time to be intimate with your spouse. An officer's spouse must learn to be inventive and creative. Touching is natural and wonderful.

Appendix C

What to Do About Fear

For the Officer:
Love Casts Out Fear

1. Please don't criticize. We are probably more critical of ourselves and your negative comments about our fears will only serve to contribute to feelings of guilt, anger and frustration.

2. Try to be empathetic and understand our problems from our point of view. If we are afraid of being home alone when you are on night shift, remember that those fears are very real to us. We need your help, support and encouragement. Perhaps installing an alarm system, purchasing a dog or even something as simple as placing an obstruction in the windows and doorways can help alleviate worry. If all the lights are on, please don't gripe about the hydro bill—accept whatever it takes to make us feel safe while you are out protecting others.

3. You are an expert on the subject of safety, so try to listen to our fears too; sharing our distress will help us cope. Believe us when we are frightened and remember that at 3:00 a.m. the imagination can go crazy.

4. Don't tell me, "You'll get used to it." The fears are persistent and a person never really gets used to loneliness and worry.

5. Remember to make a quick call if you are late or ask a fellow officer who is not too busy to do it for you. Their spouses have

the same worries and fears. We need to be reassured.

6. Don't trivialize our feelings. The fear of losing someone you love is NOT TRIVIAL.

7. Take good care of yourself, physically, mentally and spiritually. We want you to be fit so that you can deal with all aspects of your job and return to us safely.

8. Remember we love you and give you all our support.

For the Spouse: Dealing With Your Fears

Worrying is normal and sometimes useful, but don't allow yourself to become a chronic worrier. The extreme worrier has nothing to gain but poor eating and sleeping habits that will hinder their well-being. Negative thinking has been proven to give rise to disease and can only produce negative results.

1. Always think positively. You *can* control the influence that anxiety and fear have over you.

2. Continue to remind yourself that your spouse is well trained and has a sixth sense that many of us have never needed to develop. It is their survival and yours. Trust their ability.

3. Learn as much as you can about your spouse's work so that you are better informed and less apt to let your imagination run wild.

4   Be as cautious speaking to a stranger about your spouse's shift as you would be about any upcoming holiday where your home could be the target. Remember if you hear an intruder, there is no one that gets a quicker response than the family of an officer.

5. Get used to the sounds around your home and get to know the people in your neighborhood. If your newspaper is delivered

at 4:00 a.m. you will recognize this as a normal sound.

6. Don't be resentful of your spouse's occupation. He has chosen a job that is often unrewarding, and trivialities such as shift work cannot be changed. Remember there are many people who work shifts or who travel for long periods of time. You are not alone.

7. If you are interested, arrange for a Ride-Along Program so that you can witness first-hand what the officer's job entails.

8. Try to put your fears aside and concentrate on your own achievements. Take a course at a local college or university, sign up for arts and crafts classes or look for a job in your area. There are many organizations that are begging for volunteer workers. Just find something that will give you a sense of personal identity.

9. Take a self-defense course. There is no one in a better position than your spouse to try your new moves on (it could even lead to a little fun).

10. Exercise, eat properly and get lots of rest. If you are nervous and uptight, visit your local library and take out a tape or book on relaxation techniques. Enrol in Yoga classes, work out at the gym or go for a long walk. It's amazing how working up a little sweat can clear the cobwebs and relieve the stress.

11. The people and situations that your spouse must deal with are a part of life that you don't normally see or wish to see. Try to maintain a good balance in the lifestyle you are creating at home so that your family can feel warm and secure.

12. Your fears are real. Do not suppress them for fear of sounding silly. Speak openly to your spouse or seek out a friend or family member who will lend you an ear. Seek a solution to your problems.

13. If you can't sleep, read a boring book on the life of a centipede or clean out all your kitchen cupboards until you are so

exhausted you can't keep your eyes open. Try a few relaxation exercises or stretches.

14. Don't infect your children with your anxieties or they will grow into worriers just like you.

15. Anxiety takes many forms. Do not hold back or build a wall to disguise your fears. You might subconsciously push your partner away by holding back your love and affection and they will be able to sense something's wrong.

16. Families like ours live more on the edge than most. Make time to make love!

17. If you feel your fears getting out of hand, seek counseling or see your doctor. Most police services offer professional assistance. Many cities and towns have a Freedom from Fear Foundation that will be glad to help. There are a number of books and audio cassettes that deal with the topic of fear.

18. Look at your lifestyle as a challenge, not a threat.

19. Remember there is nothing that heals so well as laughter, and there is nothing to fear but fear itself.

A Prayer for the Safety of Police Officers

Oh Almighty God
Whose great power and eternal
Wisdom embrace the universes,
Watch over all police and
Law enforcement officers.
Protect them from harm
In the performance of their duty
To stop crime, robberies, riots and violence.

We pray, help them keep our streets
And homes safe day and night.

Cops Don't Cry

We recommend them to your loving care
Because their duty is dangerous.
Grant them your unending strength and
Courage in their daily assignments.
Dear God, protect these brave men and women.
Grant them your almighty protection.
Unite them safely with their families
After duty has ended.
Amen.

Author unknown

Appendix D

Success in Relationships

For the Officer:
All You Need Is Love

There is absolutely nothing as wonderful as loving someone and there is no doubt that working at a relationship and raising a family need commitment and hard work. No one can dispute the emotional burdens and hardships that an officer contends with and it is just those negative aspects that could choke the happiness from your family and eventually destroy it. Don't let your career control you.

Love and Devotion

Love is...
Slow to suspect—quick to trust,
Slow to condemn—quick to justify,
Slow to offend—quick to defend,
Slow to expose—quick to shield,
Slow to reprimand—quick to forbear,
Slow to belittle—quick to appreciate,
Slow to demand—quick to give,
Slow to provoke—quick to help,
Slow to resent—quick to forgive.

Author unknown

1. Work is work. Home is home. Learn to leave your work behind. Your home is a place for you to relax and enjoy family and friends. We need your attention too.

2. Learn good communication skills. Tell us if you've had a bad day. Your family needs to know what's bothering you or we don't know how to help. If you're not comfortable telling us right now, just be honest and let us know that. We can take it.

3. Trust your family. We are not out to 'get' you. We do not deal with the darker side of humanity and don't understand sometimes why you think the way you do. You may feel we are living in a cocoon, but thankfully it's a safe one that you have provided. We do not need to be subjected to all the horrors you see, but we do need to understand and possibly be exposed to some of them to appreciate what you deal with.

4. Don't be overprotective and suspicious. The worries you have about your family are very valid and we all worry about people we love. But not all of us get attacked in the parking lot of a mall, not all children smoke or take drugs, and not all people have affairs. Be cautious but don't be obsessive, or we'll begin to feel guilty about things we've never done or even thought about, and might begin avoiding you.

5. Appreciate. Recognize us for the work we put into the relationship. It has not been easy for us to understand you at times, or to endure the changes in you, and to brave the loneliness and fear we've felt. Tell us that you appreciate us and show us with a flower, a kiss and some of your undivided attention. Appreciate life. You of all people should be thankful to be alive and loved.

6. Don't lose your cool. If you've had a bad day, please don't take it out on us. We can help make it better by allowing you to feel comfortable at home and ease some of your worries.

7. Keep laughing. Don't ever lose that sense of humor. It lets us know that you can still see life in a positive light. It's been said that laughter can reduce the susceptibility to physical illness and disease by releasing healing hormones, so laugh…it's free.

8. Be there for us. We know you can't always be physically home for us, but call if you're not too busy just to let us know you care, and so that we can share the little joys in our lives.

9. Make time. Even if life becomes busy and complicated, make time to be with us. We need you too, and we especially need to spend time together so that we can enjoy the wonderful qualities that attracted us to each other from the beginning.

10. My friends are your friends. Get to know other friends. They may not share in the same 'shop talk' and may not even understand the way you think sometimes, but they'll accept you just the way you are.

11. Show interest. Our job may not be as exciting as yours but what we do is just as important to us. What the kids do is very important to them too. Listen to us when we need to share our problems and our thoughts.

12. Don't humiliate us. We are not criminals and do not want to be treated as such. Leave the control at work. We deserve the same amount of respect, if not more, that you demand from the public.

13. Never, ever become abusive. Mental or physical abuse is the quickest way to kill any relationship and to destroy a person's self-esteem. If you are angry, learn to channel it in a more constructive manner. Never allow your temper to get the best of you.

I finally packed and left. I was sick of his talking down to me and pushing me around like I was some criminal off the street. I knew he was frustrated and had a hard time separating work from home, but that wasn't my fault. I didn't know how to help him and I was afraid things would get worse. My leaving shocked him enough to force him to seek help. Eventually we both went to counseling together. It was the scariest thing I've ever been through.

14. Listen to your instincts. You have the wonderful gift of a finely tuned sixth sense. Use that gift on yourself. If you are feeling stress, please listen to the signs. If you find you are being disciplined more often at work, if you've incurred more sick days than usual, more injuries on the job, if your level of efficiency has decreased, if you find you are becoming more dependent on drugs or alcohol, or you are emotionally withdrawing, irritable or overly anxious, if you can't sleep or have problems eating, please, please realize these can be signs of stress.

15. Listen to those who want to help you. We are the closest to you and the first to recognize if you need help. Please listen to us and allow us to guide you in the right direction. It is not a sign of weakness to seek help. We will be here to support and love you.

16. Look after yourself. Learn to say no; you can't please everyone. Take time to relax by yourself. Take time to be with your family—they are great at uplifting the soul. Go on a holiday together. Your expected mortality rate is 57; don't be the one to fall into that category. Make sure you find time to exercise and eat properly and you will be with us for a long, long time. Don't forget how important it is to play.

This ad was sent by a police officer who was having difficulty finding a companion to fill the heavy requirements of living in a police relationship. He had been through a horrible divorce that left him with low self-esteem and a drinking problem. He missed the warmth and sharing of a serious relationship but was afraid he'd run into the same problem again. He knows the high expectations required of a partner, so he decided to run an ad in the couples section of the town newspaper. He was sure it wouldn't bring a single interested party. Here's what he wrote:

Looking for a companion who is willing to give more than 100% to the relationship.

Who is intelligent, independent and committed.

Has the ability to be organized but still flexible.

Possesses the virtue of patience.

It is essential she is understanding.

Is loving, warm and compassionate.

Loves to live precariously.

She does not have to be experienced but must be willing to learn.

Only one condition: Loves me for who I am.

Signed: A person who has a lot of love to offer and a police officer.

He received 23 responses, 20 of them from women who had been married to or dated other police officers!

The Police Department

The police department plays a very large part in assisting an officer to maintain a healthy attitude toward work. Many departments are beginning to develop programs to educate officers and their spouses about the effects the police career has on the family.

- Police departments need to provide mandatory programs for officers and their families from recruitment to retirement. This can serve as a powerful tool in producing officers who are efficient and dedicated. It is an effective way of dealing with the impact the officer's career will have on the relationship.

- Some departments hold marriage workshops and seminars to help support the spouse. This serves as a positive way of demonstrating the department's support of marriage and family.

- There are spousal groups available through some associations that serve as an informative and social way of sharing problems and concerns about this 'high-risk lifestyle'. The department needs to encourage these groups to grow. An educated and supportive spouse can only be a blessing.

- Departments must be more aware of marital problems within the police department. They need to find ways to help families through difficult times.

- The department can arrange social events where families can get together so they feel a part of the officer's career.

- The department should implement a mandatory ride-along program for all police spouses. This would allow them to experience what the officer faces during the course of his duty.

The Employee Assistance Program offers continued support by providing counseling to the officer and family for work-related and legal matters, and family, marital and financial problems. They will assist them with retirement, alcohol and substance abuse, emotional and psychological problems, and post-shooting and -incident trauma. To provide an efficient method of support the department should:

- offer the Employee Assistance Program, in which a police officer or family member can call either a counselor or a volunteer at any time of day or night.

- make sure all stations are familiar with the people involved in the Employee Assistance Program and are able to provide information upon request.

Vali Stone, author of *Cops Don't Cry*, was born in Toronto, Ontario, and now resides in Newmarket with her husband Paul, a police constable with Toronto Police Service, and their two children, Michelle and Trevor. A graduate of York University, she has published poetry, written a weekly newspaper column, and is a regular contributor to a police magazine.

Vali has formed support groups and worked intensively with police spouses to better understand the dynamics of the police family. She has developed a wellness program for police departments and speaks at conferences throughout Canada and the United States.

...my wife and I both agree Cops Don't Cry *offers valuable insight into some of the complex issues involved in a police marriage. Vali's book has become a valuable resource for myself as an instructor, and will certainly be recommended reading for police recruit training, and as well for anyone considering a police career.*

Shane Leathem, Recruit Instructor
Justice Institute for British Columbia

I would like to support Vali's realism and easy style. Her book can be a catalyst to promote self-awareness and dialogue in families and divisions and does begin to clarify expectations for new officer-families.

Nancy Hopgood, Clinical Director, DRCISST

For the past 15 years I've served as chaplain to the Windsor Police Service. In my work as chaplain I've encountered a number of people who've benefited greatly from reading this book. With our chief's approval, we are distributing a copy of Cops Don't Cry *to each new constable at their swearing-in ceremony.*

Chuck Congram, St. Andrews

Creative Bound Inc. 1-800-287-8610 www.creativebound.com

CREATIVE BOUND

Books that inspire, help and heal

DR. MAGGIE MAMEN

Laughter, Love & Limits
Parenting for Life

With warmth, wisdom and wit, Dr. Maggie Mamen (author of *Who's in Charge: A Guide to Family Management*) explores the various myths associated with parenting, and creates a general parenting philosophy with three main goals:

#3 Loving children enough to set reasonable limits until they can set limits of their own;

#2 Giving ourselves, as parents, permission to be leaders in the family;

#1 Showing our children that there is hope for the future.

The result is an approach that is useful for children of any age, from the cradle, through the teen years and beyond. *Laughter, Love & Limits* provides support and reassurance in the most important job anyone can ever undertake: Parenting for Life!

ISBN 0-921165-54-4 $18.95 CAN
208 pages $15.95 US

Ben Kubassek
author of the bestseller
SUCCEED WITHOUT BURNOUT

Five "F" Words that will Energize Your Life

Five "F" Words That Will Energize Your Life
Simple steps to move your life from Burnout to Balance

In response to the success of his bestseller *Succeed Without Burnout*, entrepreneur, author and professional speaker Ben Kubassek explores the five "F"s of Fitness, Family, Friends, Finances and Faith, and takes a deeper look at these essential ingredients of a happy, fulfilled and balanced life.

ISBN 0-921165-61-7 $16.95 CAN
184 pages $12.95 US

Call to order: **1-800-287-8610** *(toll-free in North America)*

or write to: **Creative Bound Inc., Box 424, Carp, Ontario, Canada K0A 1L0**